How To Get Your Kid To Like Math

Ken Ring

ISBN: 978-0-86467-000-7

To Claire Aumonier
My very good friend over many years

Table Of Contents

Too often, we give children answers to remember rather than problems to solve.

- Roger Lewin

WHO IS THIS BOOK FOR?

You can't *get* your child to like math. I don't really know if we have a right to get them to like anything. There is only one reasonably sure way they may become interested in this subject - and that is if you are interested in it.

There are, to the disgust of the rest, some parents and kids who already love math. It is a fact of life though, that people of all ages and in great numbers hate the very thought of it, think there's something crook about it, lie awake at night and sweat over it, and can't understand how some get it and others don't. Perhaps you were one of those kids.

You might remember coming home from school and all that nagging about doing your homework. As if that was going to improve the situation. You probably said "Why do I have to do this?" and they said "Because it's good for you, These are your best years, Get a good education and you'll thank us later, blah-blah..." It made little sense. And what about the double standard - they didn't bring work home, did they? yet you were made to do homework.

If you hated math as a kid you would have been forced to watch pasty-faced nerds in class all day, getting things right and getting ahead. Didn't they have a life? Yet people said, why couldn't you be like Ronald, or Sharon, and try a little harder. Well if you *weren't* trying for all these years, what did they think you were doing?

It was somewhat of a mystery. You knew the ones good at math didn't go home and do math right till they went to bed. You even played with them, on the weekends too, and you knew they had just as much free time as you.

The 'easy-to' books were useless - they were really hard to follow. Each "new curriculum" was supposed to be a New Deal but turned out to be, yeah, Big Deal. At the end of the day you still had the same old boring teachers with their boring voices and giving you work they even hated doing themselves.

Mostly when you were told anything in the math class you didn't remember it. When you hated math your sub-functioning mind forgot everything instantly.

Your mum and dad got you private coaching and bought you little simple books and went up to the school on PTA nights and sat around with the teacher discussing what they could all do with you. Of course *everyone* (especially those of the opposite sex who you wanted rather desperately to impress) knew you were just about bottom in the class. We all know the adults in these parent evenings weren't all sitting around cracking jokes to each other. They were feeling good about themselves, discussing how dumb you were. All in a very kind and caring way, supposedly. And all for your own good.

You know that the teacher probably said, "He's just wasting his own time and everyone else's." "He has so much potential!" "We all know he can do better." And mum would have said "What can we do? What do you suggest?" And your dad was probably considering getting tough. Right.. same dad who told you he used to get caught for smoking behind the bike sheds.

You were sitting at home babysitting the little ones while they were ganging up on you down at the school hall. When you hated math you didn't need teachers and parents gossiping about it all to everyone. You knew you weren't achieving; you didn't have to keep being reminded.

But wasn't there more to life than being able to find cube roots? If you were stuck in the bush for three days, what good would knowing how to convert to base three do? Wouldn't you be better off knowing how to make a fire?

Then there were the people who came to the house and asked you how's school. You either had to lie and make up stuff or tell the truth and say not all that good actually. "Oh dear," they'd say, looking down. There was no end in sight, and whatever you wanted to do when you left school apparently required math but things weren't going to change in the foreseeable soon.

Then when you looked around you, you realised that most of your mates hated math too. What did that tell you? Was this just a freak class of retards or a typical class in a typical year? You might have then asked yourself, as I did, have kids *mainly* hated math?

AMAZING FACT 1:
Most kids think they are lousy at math. Most kids grow up. Therefore most adults think they are lousy at math. But most adults have fairly good jobs - doctors, dentists, taxi drivers, property owners, printers, builders. Which means they get by without the math they are all supposed to be hating.

So obviously being dumb at math doesn't make a scrap of difference to being able to live in the world successfully. That is quite a strange thought. Never mind what they try and tell you, from parents to teachers to the neighbours and visitors whom you don't even know because they're friends of your mother's and would be better off minding their own business anyway - you don't actually *need* math to get by, to be an okay person and to feel good about yourself.

AMAZING FACT 2:
Most adults don't know their times tables. These are people who have been forced to learn times-tables off by heart for years and years and years because when they were at school they had to do little tests every day in what was called basic facts and mental arithmetic. And they get mad if *you* don't know your tables. But do they know theirs? Sometimes they have to think about it and work it out or look them up. Or use a calculator. Anyone can do that. Yet they'll still tell you that you must learn your tables. Why? It didn't work for them. They still don't know it and they learnt it. But they get by. So Amazing Fact 2 is that if you stop cramming in all those times-tables, you'll still probably live a successful life..

AMAZING FACT 3:

No-one seems to be entirely sure what math is. Try this on your next adult friend. Ask them, "What would you say math is? I'm interested, what would be your definition?"

If they say "It's measurement," you'd be right in thinking *Oh well I'm good at that;* if they say "Numbers," you can think *Okay, I know numbers.* If they say "It's getting things right like questions and problems," you can go *Uh huh, I answer most questions people ask me, and I can sort through problems fairly painlessly as they arise.* And if they say "Oh, it's what is in math books," you might ask, "*So if something mathematical is in some other book does that mean it's not math? Because if what you're saying is math then I was always fairly good at it, but I was not according to all my teachers and my parents at the time..*

So Amazing Fact 3 is that if no-one knows what math is, then no-one can be bad at it.

When people don't know what math is they just make up whatever suits them: like "it's 'measuring' isn't it, size, shape, symbols, numbers, calculations" - but you do all these all the time, without any hassle. You do a calculation every time you cross the road.

If they were to really look at the origin of the word 'mathematics', .

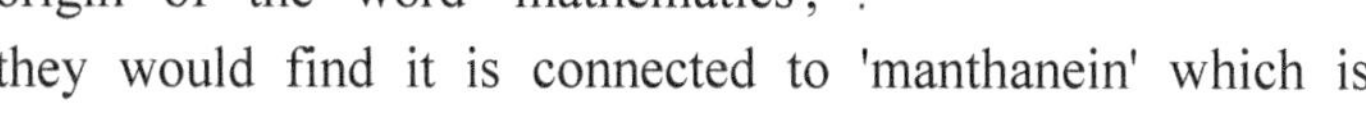
they would find it is connected to 'manthanein' which is

Greek for 'learning', and 'madras' which meant 'master' and also is the root for the word 'mad'. So does math come from a mad master?

Because no-one knows what it is, they set themselves little tests; basic facts, mental arithmetic, exams, mathex competitions, all to try to find out who the top dogs are. But competition does not create quality, it creates winners and losers. The losers, and there are heaps more of them, are called failures, even though they like numbers outside of school, measure like crazy when they build hot-rods and things, design shapes in clothes and houses and navigate 100% successfully everywhere they go (or they wouldn't get there) and they even get there on time! But they still think and are told they are no good at math.

In my MATHMAN mathemagic shows I am forever getting kids up out of the audience to act as assistants. I do not know these kids, I have never seen them before. Consequently I don't know the ability or intelligence of the child getting up to help. I just pick them out of a sea of eager faces. Yet I have never yet struck a kid who is not bright! This is incredible to me - every kid I ask up is switched on and up with the play, ready to catch me out should I make a deliberate-on-purpose mistake. Doesn't this say something about how we artificially categorize each other? It can't be coincidence that I always strike the bright ones.

I think we need to stop beating kids over the head with things we adults think is going to be good for them, when we adults very often hate the sight of it ourselves. Philosophers have been saying for centuries that math is about life itself, which has to be so much more than boring arithmetic. Math is about our mind, our loves, and the way we think and work. Math has been described as the wonder of beauty and the beauty of wonder.

In these pages there's not much arithmetic, or quick calculating methods, or base changes. I'll save that for a later volume. This book is for those who at the moment have been temporarily turned off to all that and are crying out for a change in perspective.

HOW TO KEEP A KID FROM LIKING MATH

A perfect way to discourage someone from enjoying math is by telling him he has to do some every day. As long as he is small enough so he is made afraid not to do it, he will sit down every day and suffer the tasks, that is, when pushed hard. When he gets big enough so you can't make him do it anymore, he'll quit. This happens to 4 out of every 5 pupils who reach the option-choosing stage at 5th form level. That's exactly what happens to 99.5% of the kids who are *made* to take it.

There are millions of kids who acquire fairly proficient skills at math, helping their parents run shops, making scale models from plan sheets, or cutting dress patterns for dolls or themselves. Then they forget how much they liked it, and later someone comes along and calls it math. "Oh that stuff - I did that as a kid."

"May I go over to Jim's house and play with his toys? Mine are all educational." Wall Street Journal

The easier it is for children to stop doing regular math, the easier it is for them to start again. If a child is having trouble, throwing money in the direction of remedial help from private tutors makes math out to be a far worse curse to the child. If he stops and starts as he chooses, he will indeed start sometimes, when he feels up to it and in his time and space. If not he will never want to start in any time or space.

You can liken it to practicing and playing a musical instrument. He will have spells of hardly playing at all, spells of being discouraged, and spells of enthusiasm in which he gains in great spurts. Eminent educator John Holt once said, "It's a very funny thing about learning - I learnt a lot about the cello in the 7 or 8 years I wasn't playing (between ages 42 and 50) I don't know what exactly it is, but when I began again, I was much more of a musician than when I stopped - I'd heard other music, I'd seen a lot of cellists, I was learning even though I never touched the cello."

Math is no different to playing an instrument or to any other activity that requires the acquiring of a skill. The purpose of teaching music is not always to produce a famous cellist or conductor. A child should be shown how to do arithmetic or to spell correctly purely if and because he shows a spark of early interest and if it obviously empowers him. If it has the reverse effect of making him powerless the activity should not be continued, any more than he should be given sleeping pills for no reason. The child himself will tell you when he is doing things of value to him. He will tell you when he has the feeling of slowly getting somewhere.

One cannot extract beauty in music from an instrument that is so cheap and bad that it cannot produce it. That is not to say anyone's brain is inferior to another's, only that the willingness might not be there, or the concentration, or it might just be that the interest *is* high, but the child is living such a full-on life that there are other interests that just happen to be higher. It doesn't mean he is necessarily poor at math.

Also we do not in this day and age expect the same doctor who examines our children's eyes and the doctor who fills their dental cavities to be the same person. So why should the class teacher be expected to be the right person to coach the delicate and sensitive material that math is, just because she happens to be there and by sheer chance your child happens to be in her class? And it's not much good saying oh well, let's put up with it for now even though he's not getting anywhere, and later on we might review the situation if it's still not working. It is like saying that you will feed your baby junk and if he grows up to be strong and healthy, then you will switch him to wholesome, nourishing food.

So to keep children on the wrong side of math, keep it boring and make sure he gets something with a black cross beside it every day. Make sure too he gets the notion that if he gets some answers wrong he is to think of himself as a bad person and a loser, not that he gets things mostly right. Make sure it's either too easy or too difficult in his mind, and he gets no firm handle on his ability. Tell him how important something is and that if he doesn't try now, it will affect him throughout the remainder of his (now useless) life. Spread the unpopularity of math, use it for punishment - as in writing out basic math facts during lunchtime, as the penalty for the terrible crime of talking to others when he was supposed to be sitting in silence working alone. And unless liking math is seen as uncool, there may be some family members who think he is weird.

Insist on him doing his homework as soon as he comes home from school and before he watches TV or goes out to play. Just because you are allowed to fall onto the lazy-boy and put your feet up when you come in the door, doesn't mean he is allowed to do that too. Double standards are the rule, and he better get used to it.

"Would the gifted children carry on quietly with the chapter on Propositional Calculus."

ARE THERE TWO MATH?

When I was a child I hated classroom math but I loved puzzles and crosswords and amazing number facts, all that number-oriented fun that I discovered outside the school. There were crosswords in magazines, puzzles in comics, and competitions on the radio and at fairground stands in the form of 'guess how many jellybeans are in this jar and you'll win a bike.'

Even at school we weren't allowed to do the fun math. We played Battleships after exams - and if we got caught we were put in detention - why? You couldn't get a better math exercise in graphing, co-ordinate plotting than Battleships - ah, but it wasn't the teacher's idea, was it! That seemed to make all the difference! So what exactly was really considered to be good math?

Well there was the math they allowed and presented at school and there was everything else. There was always a handful of bright kids who could do the school stuff and all the rest who couldn't. Obviously there were two math, maybe even more. The one in school and the one outside. I kept quiet about it because kids do, they're scared enough anyway and don't want to rock a boat which already tips over unaided.

When later I went into teaching, I deliberately didn't teach math the old boring ways although I was supposed to and required to. In fact my grading as a teacher loomed and I hadn't included any regular math lesson planning. The stated fact that I didn't want to upset the children impressed nobody. The upshot was that I still taught and did math in class but I didn't ever call it anything because it became math for a reason, math only for application when a need arose. My teaching career didn't last.

"No, Billy, the difference between 10 and 6 is not a rather gray area."

It's ironic to me that nowadays I go from school to school doing math presentations and calling it that too. My joy is overhearing kids leave the show saying That was really neat! or 'I didn't know a math lesson could be like *that.*

But you could do anything and call it math. Everything that happens in the world involves direction, measurement, shape, some idea of number, and a relativeness due to the impact of proportion or contrast. Nothing is math-free. Whatever anyone is interested in at any time does contain math. You might as well accept it - everyone is good at it. Not only that, you were good at math when you were just a baby and couldn't talk yet. When your mother held a spoon with some baby mush or fetid object on it she said "More?" (or, "here comes the aeroplane!") and your little mouth opened. You understood 'more' before you could actually talk. You understood 'No' too, and indicated such by shaking your head. 'No', of course means, mathematically speaking, no more, or less of more. This is a math concept and contains an understanding of "is not equal to.".

Because the dynamics of math are absorbed very early it is probably not that the child doesn't understand the processes if he thinks he's no good at math. When the child fell over he learnt about gravity and down. When he bumped into walls he learnt about impact and deceleration and the need to distinguish between forward and backward as available movement alternatives. When stacked blocks fell after a certain height had been reached he rediscovered the Theory of Limits, 500 years after Kepler first proposed calculus as a way of understanding the orbits of planets.

Then, when stacking blocks he learnt about adding, and subtraction before that when the breast was taken away sooner than he wished, multiplication when too much happened too quickly, and division when he discovered he was required to share things with other children. The last two took the longest to grasp.

These processes were interpreted egocentrically. If there is no verbal labelling in the home as things happen, it all comes in a rush when the child enters school and is told every process must be now be called something. The homes with lots of talk produce kids who have less trouble with math-understanding, not meaningless babble and arguing but real talk between parent and child - helpful and patient answering of 'why' questions. Otherwise they get to school and immediately start lagging behind the others who do have communicative home life. At early school the kid finds math is just a way of talking about the world - *like we do at home.* School quickly becomes a river which sweeps the child up in its current. You sink or swim, and fast.

YOU IN KINDERGARTEN

Robert Fulghun wrote ' all I ever need to know I learned in kindergarten.' Wisdom, he said, is really in the sandpit at Sunday school. These are the things you learn in this environment:

- sharing everything
- playing fair
- not hitting people
- putting things back where you found them
- not taking things that aren't yours
- cleaning up your own mess
- saying you're sorry when you hurt somebody
- washing your hands before you sit down and eat
- flushing the loo
- how warm milk and cookies are good for you
- living a balanced life that includes learning some and thinking some and drawing and painting and singing and dancing and playing and working a little every day
- taking a nap every afternoon
- watching for traffic, holding hands and staying together
- being aware of wonder

- remembering the little seed in the foam cup - the roots go down and the plant goes up and nobody knows why, but we are all like that. Goldfish and guinea pigs and seeds die, so do we.
- remembering early reading books and the first word you learned
- the biggest work of all - LOOK

Everything you need to know is in there somewhere. The Golden Rule, love, basic sanitation, ecology, politics, equality and sane living. Take any one of those items and extrapolate it into sophisticated adult terms and you can apply it to your family life or your work or your government, and it holds true and clear and firm. Think what a better world it would be if we all - the whole world - had cookies and milk about three o'clock every afternoon and then lay down for a nap. Or if all the governments had as a basic policy to always put things back where they found them and to clean up their own mess. And it is still true, no matter how old you are - when you go out into the world it is best to hold hands and stick together.

These are the early underpinning math concepts and a knowledge of them prepares the child for anything which comes later. The concepts are one thing at a time, one on one, what combinations look like and how they 'work' together, and this is about patterns of behavior and the confidence that grows gradually with the expectation of perception.

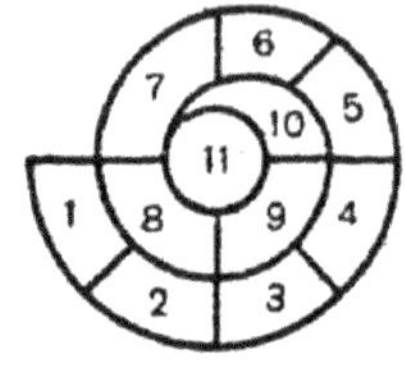

GETTING AN ATTITUDE

I bet you're a hard working parent, one that wants the best for your kids. Because you are that type of conscientious person, you probably work hard at your job. It follows that you probably come home tired, flop in the chair and think 'I'm home, phew, what a day'. When someone says 'Have a good day dear?' you say, 'Oh man, what a day. I'm exhausted.' And you don't feel like talking about it. You don't want to 'bring work home'. Yet we don't often allow our children this right. We expect children to be keen to go to school, to be excited about the learning process, and to bring work home, which we even label *home*work.

If they don't enjoy any of this we think they have some 'learning difficulty'. Perhaps those kids have a parenting difficulty, because we, the parents, in our misdirected wisdom and ignorance of how we ourselves behave, teach them to resent their day through role-modelling of our after-work-behavior. When we show them we resent what has been *our* day we unwittingly teach them to resent school.

If we go to work and our attitude is oh, it's just a job, then kids will feel that too. If a teacher feels that, her children will see everything as uphill grind. Unpaid, too. Slaves can't be expected to be happy about their lot.

Imagine two different households. In the first, the parent behaves as above - comes in, flops, wants to say very little about his day at work, wants instead to 'spend time with the kids' which never really happens because he/she is too tired. Sound familiar? But imagine a fictitious second case, where the parent comes home and starts leaping about excitedly, saying to anyone who wants to listen, "I've had such a great day today! I've learnt so much!! I just can't wait to get back there tomorrow and learn a whole lot of new stuff! These are the most exciting days of my life!"

Children of the first household are going to role-model negative attitudes about spending their day, and there is no way they are going to find school in any way exciting. Their home attitude role-modelling process presents what their daily expectancy is going to be. What's more, that factor will override anything good that actually does happen at school.

But children of the second household are going to be excited about going to school. It goes a whole lot further. School is just a part of the general excitement they will have about living and exploring the world and themselves.

How many houses do you know that are like the second type? What about yours?. The stresses and pressures of living in this day and age get to you very quickly and before you know it you become a depressed personality. I do not believe we have the right to tell kids to be happy and excited if we are not like that ourselves. Yet most of us seem to raise this double standard high. Perhaps we didn't have the opportunities in life that we perceive kids of today have. I don't know that that is a valid reason to really make damn sure our kids aren't going to miss out. Because then we work hard and expect them to work hard and expect them to be grateful we are providing this opportunity for them, to make something of themselves. But kids don't see it that way. Kids just see the double standard.

It is perfectly understandable You can't show them something as graphically obvious as a double standard and then tell them not to recognize it. Kids can't help but absorb that double standard for themselves too. They will split themselves in half. And they will just resent you for it without even knowing. How do they split themselves in half? One part of them says I am loved, I am cared for and the other says I am a failure, I am unworthy, I can't do this stuff.

The parents who are the most loving and caring in their hearts yet who are the most miserable in their own work places, are the ones who will cause this split the most in their children. And that means most adults today. Which is why learning difficulties are so widespread, why the schools just aren't working, and why we are producing disgruntled aimless youth with drug and alcohol problems. A divided person is one warring with himself. As a part of that warring he will self-abuse, if not now then later in life when crises present.

THE CURE

The cure is - to get happy. Drop your job if you don't like it. Live an exciting life, whatever it takes, and it may mean a wage cut for a while. Live a dream, take a step toward the light, even if it is just one step and the light is just from a new doorway opening.

You owe it to yourself and your children. This could be the greatest thing you can give them, over and above material things. By showing them that you so love and respect yourself that you are willing to make sacrifices in order to become a more contented inner person, you are giving them the tools to make them happy too. This is the real education, not schools, not books, not money, not helping them with their homework. Of course all that helps too, but without the role model of contentment the rest is a poor second.

I mix with many home-school families. I have found that this attitude is especially to be found in those homes. Because parents and kids mix and mingle all day together, children in this environment are totally exposed to the parents' life and attitudes. Most home-school families see the whole venture as something exciting anyway, and parents and children all get involved in each other's pet projects. They are forever trotting off to libraries or going to exhibitions or just hanging out at places where they know they will find some useful result. Parents and children in this way re-learn to love their lives, get back into exploring the unknown and have fun together, which some believe is what you have children for.

Home-schooling can have a huge effect on their language development. The first word my infant son said was 'moon', but the second was 'excavator'. At a home-school camp where I was the entertainment one year, I asked a passing child to quickly tell me a number. He said, "What are my options?" So I said, "Well, give me a large number." "I can't," he said, "numbers are all the same size. It's the values that are different." I stood corrected. They are. It took a five year old to teach me to think more carefully before I spoke. That kid will go far because he clearly came from a home that regularly challenged ideas. And he was a pleasant kid, not nasty or cheeky.

I know we can't all home school, but at least we can get into modes of life that afford us relative tranquility, so our children can learn to grapple with sophisticated concepts in a stress-free way.

MATH LESSON - CHEATING

Suppose you want to find something out, and you know that your next door neighbor Mr. Jones will know it because he is an expert in that area.

We could think of three options:

1. You sit in your chair and say nothing, thinking about the problem. This is the Contemplation - Work-it-out-for-yourself-and-you'll-be-better-off-in-the-long-run Strategy.
2. You could sit in your chair and say aloud 'I wonder what blah-blah' and do nothing about it, thinking about the problem, and vow to ask Jones next time you see him. This is the Announce-The-Problem-and-Then-Work-It-Out Strategy
3. You could stand up and announce "Bob will know. I'm going next door right now and he'll tell me the answer." This is a quick short-cut, some would even say cheating. It's getting the answer from someone smarter than yourself.

Let's assume your kids have been sitting playing on the rug and can witness all three options above. There is only one option that will teach them anything about math problem-solving that is of any real use. It's the Cheating Strategy.

Am I advocating laziness? Yes. Am I recommending deceit? No. The bottom line is always getting the answer, to solving something. In math the end always justifies the means.

If you are at the supermarket and want to know the price of a packet of biscuits, you approach the checkout girl and ask her. Holding the pricelist in her hand, she doesn't shut her eyes and say 'Let me try and work it out,' nor does she get a pencil and make a few calculations. No, she looks up the answer. If you take your car to the mechanic and he can't find the problem he either asks somebody or he looks up the manual.

Is this cheating? Most would call it common sense. If there's a resource person around you would be dumb not to go and ask that person the answer. This is what happens in the world at large. So why shouldn't it happen in math? If the answers are at the back of the book you might as well go and look them up. That's not cheating. Otherwise what are libraries for? Why do people compile dictionaries? Why have Citizens' Advice Bureaus, and why ask a policeman for directions?

Some might say, oh, if the answers are at the back of the book and you're allowed to look them up, kids will do that all the time. My reply is, they won't, any more than you go immediately to the back page of a murder mystery to see who did it rather than read the story through. The point is, if you are interested in the story you will test your conclusion and wait for the end. It's the same with math. If you are interested in testing yourself you will try and work it out for yourself. And if you are not interested you might as well go look up the answer, because you're not going to try very hard to work it out anyway.

I say cheating is a fair strategy but it is misnamed. We slap that word 'cheating' on a reliable problem-solving method. What's wrong with whispering to the person next to you in class, "Hey, Jimmy, what's the answer to number 23?" "It's $56.75." "Thanks." Adults call this teamwork. What's wrong with working in groups, even in groups of two?

The situation is that you have a problem and you know who has the answer and you know that if you go over to that person he will supply it gladly. Remember, in my first example case; having announced loudly what you propose to do, up you get and go over to Jones's. You find the answer, you come back, and you announce again "That worked well!! He told me!!"

A child watching this would have no difficulty absorbing this as a problem-solving strategy. The regular steps involved are:

a) Identify the problem to be solved,
b) Admit you need help and share this with the group.
c) Openly share what you propose as a plan of action, in case the group has other suggestions,
d) Approach the resource person with your request for assistance and
e) Come back with the answer and let the group share in what proved to be a successful strategy.

All these steps are important, being the structure of

problem-solving strategy. Unless children see adults doing it in its entirety, they won't absorb this strategy as a tool in their own arsenal. But how often do we ponder a problem and sit and stew over it, thinking that we're supposed to work things out for ourselves, rather than go an easier route. There are social spinoffs too, better than the lonely path of personal frustration.

If we don't display this strategy often as a family way of going about things, children won't learn problem-solving. They will sit there pondering insolvable problems, both at home and in class, suffering in silence surrounded by resource people but not accessing them, because they have not had a better role modelling situation. And in its very absence there is a worse role model - one that says if you get up and ask you're cheating, and so respite from inner conflict runs counter to intelligence and ability. In fact a teacher might say, "Haven't you read the instructions? I told you what to do, didn't I? How many times must I tell you before it sinks in? I've told you a hundred times. Go away and work it out".

A lot of teachers don't know what they're there for. They think they're there to teach. Wrong. They think they're there to 'facilitate'. Wrong. They are not there for anything other than to be a correct role model and a clear communicator. "Do your *own* work but come to *me* if you need any help" is valid but is said badly. What you mean is, try to work it out but I am here if you get stuck.

It's what you are that the student notices, not what you do. Are you a person the student sees going and getting answers from somewhere or are you a person who just sits at a desk giving out commands or stands in front of a blackboard talking? How are you handling *your* difficulties?

How can you, the parent be a role model for personal difficulties? When I was 13 and beginning to wonder about girls, my father came into my room blurted out to me, "Do you think about girls?" He was as embarrassed as I was. I picked up immediately on his embarrassment and I vehemently said no. The fact was that my thoughts were about the opposite sex, and I did not know if that was okay. Now I had to hide it from my dad. Before, I had one problem - now I had two.

When my own son reached the same age I decided I wasn't going to repeat that mistake. If he was going to share any personal problems at all, he wasn't going to do it if I *told* him to - it would only work if I shared my problems first. When we were together of an evening in our spa pool. I just spoke to him about matters of concern to me, in business dealings, friendships, and then I angled myself around to personal problems. What I was doing was putting in place an atmosphere in which personal problems could be aired. It took about three weeks, and then he too started sharing his personal life. I'm certain it would never have happened if I had blurted out something like "TELL ME ANY PROBLEMS YOU'RE HAVING."

It's exactly the same with math. Math problems quickly become personal ones because they knock confidence and they symbolize mental traps and being stuck. When teachers say to children. 'Come to me and ask if you have any difficulties' or when the parent says 'Look, I 'm here anytime, you know that,' these are well-intentioned but rarely have the desired effect. What is the alternative?

As a community we should all be coming together and talking and doing together things. Those who offend against society are those marginalized by education practices that have excluded them. Government moneys have been poured in such that sociologists and psychologists have been studying all this for many years now. And what have they come up with? For all their recommendations more studies keep ensuing. Why aren't they telling us there is no need any more for any child to suffer any problem by himself?

When you do things as a group, a marvelous thing happens - a role modelling process occurs, in which the group becomes how you see *yourself,* because you are always a bunch of inner voices operating as a team. Only then can a child think for himself and work out things in isolation, but not before. And solitariness is always optional - rather than some teacher ordering an individual to go off and work something out on his own, it should be that the group is always there and the individual decides to go off by himself for his own reasons.

There is an old joke that goes:

"How many legs does a donkey have?"

"Four."

"Okay, how many legs has a donkey if you call its tail another leg?"

"Five."

"Wrong. A donkey only has four legs; it doesn't matter what you call them."

In math we are talking about thinking and how to use thinking to get somewhere. Not 'lateral' thinking either. It's all just thinking. You use what you can, with what you've got, where you are. That's what happens. There's you and the world, and both have to fit together. They do, or either you or it wouldn't be here.

Cheating, in the sense of unnaturalness, never comes into it. You have a right to be on this earth and a right to quick and easy and painless ways of doing things, if you can see how to achieve them. Cheating is only a no-no if someone else is going to suffer. But if you ask someone for an answer, like a teacher, how are they suffering? Especially if they're glad to be of help. Especially if that's what they're paid to be there for.

MATH LESSON - LYING

Suppose I hold up one finger. "Imagine this is one elephant." I unfold another finger. "How many now?" Two. "Now another. How many now?" Three! "No, none!"

These are fingers, not elephants. I was lying, something we do in math to find out, say, something about numbers of elephants. We use things like fingers or marks on paper to aid our brain, otherwise we'd have to go to the zoo and get real elephants to stand *in a line on our hand* so that we could count them. That should be obvious, but it's not.

Math books, like advertisements, are often written by people who are liars. In the example opposite the shoes are not half price at all. In life two quarts of alcohol added to two quarts of water do not give two quarts of liquid. A book might say, "3 men are digging a field. How many men will it take to dig 2 fields?" You can put the textbook down and look out the window like I used to do as a kid and you might think well, there are no men digging the field. This book must be lying.

Believe it or not there are some children who worry about what they have been told are lies and cheating and who haven't been informed that math clicks along quite happily at these levels.

I believe children make mistakes, often because they can't see the dividing line between pretending and lying. Nor can they see the dividing line between making mistakes and doing things by trial and error. They are told lying and mistakes are wrong. They are simultaneously told that pretending (drama) and risk-taking are worthy behaviors.

People generally still don't see the value of shortcuts to get what they want. Because they have done a thing all their lives in one way, they are resistant to newness. We are more enlightened now about our gregarious needs. But adults still don't let kids copy each other because it's considered cheating, and one of the very reasons kids hate math is because they are denied the opportunity to talk to each other during it. Why shouldn't math *always* be a group activity? Don't we all learn from each other? If not, what's the fashion industry all about?

If you want to do an experiment to see how grown adults copy each other, go into a hospital ward at night where the patients are sleeping, and cough. In five minutes the whole ward will be coughing. Or stand in a crowded elevator and scratch your face. Everyone will have itchy faces too. The only place that the concept of 'cheating' has is in industrial espionage and breaches of copyright; hardly part of the child's world. We adults obviously never grow out of the need to copy each other, so we should allow that habit and joy amongst children, instead of punishing them when they look at their neighbor's work.

So math itself is not above telling lies. We are supposed to be conscious of accuracy and precision, and of the notion of non-negotiable results. But at times math says one thing and means another. It uses a word like 'multiply' which the dictionary says means 'to get more in quantity.. to increase'. And doesn't the Bible say Go forth and multiply? Well, what about multiplying by one? Things stay the same. The Bible does not say Go forth and stay the same. Multiplying by a fraction? Things diminish. Multiplying by zero? Things get eliminated. (Shall we add murder to cheating and lying?).

There is often more than one possible answer. Multiply doesn't just mean one thing. The preciseness of the result depends on the accuracy of the question.. Does anyone say the question is wrong? No, we would say in this case confusing. Well, answers can be confusing too. There are often two answers depending on what the frame of reference is. What is two plus two and a half? It could be four and a half or six. You can look at a doorway and say that it is a rectangle. But it isn't. It nearly is, though, but no carpenter is perfect.

Right and wrong are not finite states. Things can be *nearly right* and *wronger*. 2 + 2 = 17 is wronger than 2 + 2 = 3.99999, which is nearly right. The trouble is, no-one is allowed to discuss these things, because no-one allows the time. If kids could talk about it more, they would be allowed to project their points of view, and after all, mistakes are very often just other options. I would concede that math endeavors to be accurate and the *approach* to accuracy is the main intention.

In line with this a teacher must have an alternative explanation for what he/she is saying. Too often teachers don't. They think because they say a thing once that should be it. But they have to have *at least* one other way of explaining something. I have many children coming to me after my shows, saying "we do say what you are telling us to say; we ask the teacher things but they get all grumpy at us."

I seem to find myself more and more these days in a situation where I am telling the children to educate their teachers. There has to be something wrong with that.

What's wrong with this ad? *Look at the date.*

MATH LESSON - STEALING

Remember how we were taught to subtract 19 from 42? We first say nine and what make two, can't do it, take a ten from the 4 and call the 2 twelve. Now 9 and what make— Er, just a minute. Take what from where? Did we ask the four if we could borrow one of its tens? No. We just took it. Just taking something is called stealing. What about cancelling out? That's stealing too, and quite ruthless.

Consider the integer 1. There it is, sitting there minding its business. Then we say 1 - 1 = 0. What are we doing? Taking a one away? No, it's still there. Actually, in 1 - 1 = 0 we aren't taking anything away really. We're adding something. What? We're adding minus one. Otherwise we wouldn't get zero. How does that work? Well, we're really starting with 1 = 1. When we add -1 to the left we must do the same to the right. The right becomes 0 because we choose to resolve it. The left does too but we leave that side as '1 - 1' just to show what we've done.

We are actually adding something whilst simultaneously something is being taken away. The equation is naturally feeling rather pleased because we are offering a gift, but all the time we are *removing* something. Isn't this stealing?

This is what is often so confusing, the knowing exactly

what is being said. If there can be confusion about 1 - 1, then all the rest is going to bring difficulties too, unless children are going to be allowed to talk about it from a philosophical point of view. And believe me they will warm to such a discussion. This is the core of real math. It is exciting because it is about life itself. It can also be very amusing sorting basic messages like this out. When they ask 'why' as children so often do, they are hooking into this world.

The best way to talk about equations is to go out and play around on the seesaw. The equals is in the middle. If you add something to one side you must do the same to the other. You can use cups of water on each side, take one away, what happens? what must you add to the other side to retain 'equals'? When someone steals something from you, what must they do to restore the balance, to square the ledger?

Because math is describing an event a good way of using experiences is to write everything down you do. Then you can come up with some basic rules. Map the event. What actually happened in the math story?. How did we report it? Make it a discussion thing. Math can be an endless talking and negotiating of these basic concepts. Once understood in their simple forms, they can be used to solve life's more complex challenges.

ADULT LESSON TIME

Do we want to ram our ideas and prejudices down children's throats or do we want them to discover what they need for their life? Are teachers interested in sharing ideas and getting heaps of new ones or is there only time to cover the curriculum and that's all?

If you want your kids to like math, you might make time available, heaps of it, to encourage the asking of questions. At the very outset, math is about enquiry, in a safe mental environment. When just a little confidence is eroded in this area, the whole child's learning brain will clam up.

Competition in the classroom, even awareness of who is not amongst the top few, can destroy confidence.. I suggested earlier that competition does not produce quality, only winners and losers. Unless the child is competing only against himself the task is hardly worthwhile.

Dr. Teresa Amabile of Brandeis University reports on a statistical exercise whereby 85 children were given collage materials and instructed to come up with individual art pieces. They were all told that prizes would be awarded. However, half the group were informed that the best would be judged by professional art experts and the other half were told a raffle would decide the winners. Professionals did indeed do the judging, unaware of the experimental nature of the exercise. Interestingly, the winning group was evenly represented from both groups, demonstrating that competition does not necessarily produce quality.

If your child says he does not like math, before anything else, ask yourself, is there a tension because he feels like a mental racehorse. Hemingway once said that at some level everything is war. War is certainly a way of achieving change, but it always produces casualties. Peace just takes longer, that's all.

War is a form of bullying. A bully is the one that *starts* the fight. Competition is mainly foistered onto children's shoulders. There is no choice in the matter. As such I would regard it as bullying. Unfortunately time is needed for anything worthwhile and lasting. Money thrown at the situation won't work. One must be able to ask, am I giving this time in my life, am I available at the *child's* pace, not that laid down by schools or norms, and not necessarily only when I feel like it, to talk about issues that may be bothering him.

One might ask, am I enthusiastic and excited about enquiry in my own life, such that I am setting a role model that will make my child an eager and alive student. If the answer is no to these, perhaps you have work to do on yourself first. No amount of remedial math at school or private coaching will fix it, because your child still will be exposed to you and your attitudes when he comes home. If you can admit that you have work to do on yourself, and your child sees you going about it, that in itself is a valuable lesson because it tells *him* that it is okay to be humble enough to seek help.

But if you say no, *I'm* not the one with the problem, your child will role model that too and could deep down resist any help whatsoever. Chances are he will resent anyone trying to tell him what to do, just like his parent.

We are always the one with the problem, because not a day goes by without something untoward occurring that needs to be addressed. You may not call that a problem, but the sooner we accept that there is always work to be done, the sooner the child will accept that too.

The trick is to make it all seem rewarding and exciting. To do that we all need a strategy of diluting the tasks so that they are manageable, taking one step at a time. This is a *very* math concept. One thing at a time is how counting operates, and sequencing in any process. Do you take one step at a time, take one day at a time? If you want your child to be okay at math you might want to take a look at your attitude to that. Otherwise your child may become the victim of overload, may withdraw from the learning environment and 'freeze' like a computer hard drive with too many windows open.

The only answer is to give time, heaps of it, whatever it takes, to be available for your child so that tasks can be shortened into bite-sized bits. If he doesn't even like sitting at a desk, let alone doing school-type-work there, it's no use making him sit there. Your immediate task is to get his toosh on that seat for a tiny time and then slowly increase that time until he's used to being there You may have to give him food there, or reward him for longer and longer periods of sitting. This all takes time. Unless you decide first of all that you are going to put in time, other well-meant efforts could fail.

EXPECTANCY

The influence of role modelling from parents is huge, and surpasses any other influences in the child's life. Parents seem relatively unaware of the importance of it. Otherwise they would not boast to friends and acquaintances within earshot of the children, "Oh yes, well I wasn't very good at math at school either, so I'm not surprised at his/her marks. It obviously runs in the family." How very potentially harmful to the child's chances of success! To be told that it is cool to be a failure in this particular household means that failure will be rewarded because it is a family tradition, whilst success will be discouraged because it will be regarded as something odd.

Expectancy is only just starting to become properly understood. In a recent experiment involving New York schools, a group of psychologists went into selected schools and told teachers in classes the same story. These children, they said (showing some class names on a list), have been selected by us for a project later in the year. They are considered exceptional in some category. And they watched from afar the academic progress of these children. Very quickly they rose to the top of their class if they weren't already amongst the top children. What they didn't tell the teachers at the outset was that the names were chosen at random.

Expectancy breeds success. It also breeds failure. Because the teachers were told that these kids were exceptional, special allowances were made for them, extra attention given them to bring them up to par, and surprise shown when they didn't perform to what the teacher reasoned should have been their true performance.

But shouldn't every child be given this amount of attention? Teachers are overworked and underpaid the world over. They just want to get through the day and go home and flop.

It was also found that those sitting at the back and side were low achievers and those sitting along the front and up the middle participated more. Something to do with the teacher's field of attention?

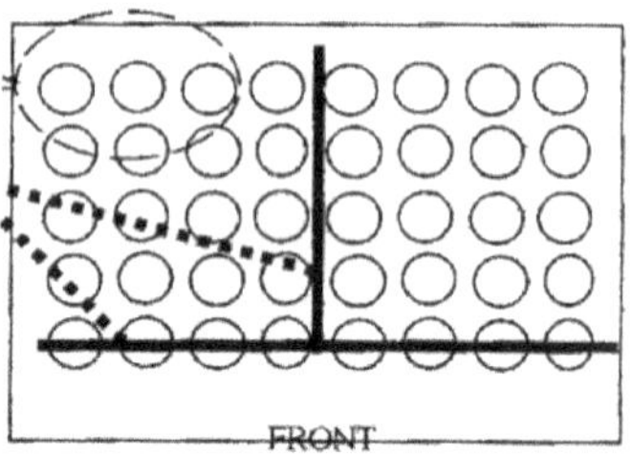

It's up to you, the parent, to provide this expectancy and this attention, and if your child thinks he is no good, perhaps it's an indication that *you* should examine how and what you are saying to him.

In the West, children have always been sacrificed in favor of the syllabus. The syllabus is society's agenda; if you don't perform you're of no use. It goes right to the top - in the British parliament, if you stand against the party tide you become a backbencher. This is the legacy of British culture.

There is a marked difference between the schools of Taiwan and the British system. Educators have long wondered why Asian students are 3 or 4 years ahead of their British counterparts in math and science by the time they get to university age. Is it the increased competition, something genetic, racial or what?

They sent a group of English professors in education on a study grant to Taiwan to have a look at their schools. Every school they visited was the same, so success was not just the result of a group of exceptional staff at just one place.

They typically saw a teacher in front of the class, talking, hands of the pupils going up, she writing math up on the board, turning back, more hands going up, more writing on the board, the usual story. As she went on, the teacher asked children questions, as teachers typically do. When she struck one child who obviously didn't know, she left her post at the front of the class and went over to that child. Meanwhile the whole class waited. In perfect and respectful silence. She took as long as was necessary to help that slower child. They all knew to wait because it could be any one of them at any time. Then she returned to the front and the whole class started up again.

That would just not happen in a western school. What does this mean for the Asian system of education? It means that all children are catered for more, because the educational philosophy is geared towards passing, not failing. That is why at the very top there is a far more qualified pool for the Asian job market, especially in math and sciences.

The English system is different. Having developed from the monastic tradition which needed to perpetuate a ruling intellectual elite, the British system was and still is geared toward cutting people out, making them fail, and hence the system of exams, the curriculum, the 'disciplines' , the "O" levels etc. The British system is a Failure Factory. At failure it has a huge success rate. This failure-industry has been refining itself for a number of years now. It should therefore come of no great surprise that learning difficulties are rare in Asian countries.

It goes further than the schools, too. In the Asian home it is seen as the parents' responsibility to prepare the school-age child for school the next day. To that end they make time available, not just to supervise homework, but to be on hand to encourage and explain if need be, and to devote time accordingly.

I do not claim that the Asian or any culture is perfect. All have flaws making them less-than-ideal societies - in Taiwan the overcrowding, the organized crime, the poverty and competition for jobs. The student suicide rate is higher. But in this educational feature they are demonstrating something to the English tradition of education which we would be silly not to take note of.

Expectancy is high in Asian homes not so much for the children to do well, but for the child to feel the support of the parents, and for the parents in turn to know the child feels that support. The teachers too seem to have the support of the community because all the children are included positively. No-one points the finger and says he or she is hopeless, useless and dumb. Consequently no child feels that stigma either and accordingly, they do better.

Parenting and teaching is always more about expectancy of support than expectancy of achievement. Achievement will follow by itself if the support is there.

A father and his son were driving to a ballgame when their car stalled on the railroad tracks. In the distance a train whistle blew a warning. Frantically, the father tried to start the engine, but in his panic he couldn't turn the key, and the car was hit by the onrushing train. An ambulance sped to the scene and picked them up. On the way to the hospital the father died. The son was still alive but his condition was very serious and he needed immediate surgery. The moment they arrived at the hospital, he was wheeled into an emergency waiting room and the surgeon came in, expecting a routine case. However, on seeing the boy, the surgeon drew away and muttered "I can't operate on this boy - he's my son."

Take a minute to figure this out before you continue reading. Did the dead father's soul get transported and reincarnated into the doctor's body? Was the boy only adopted?

When you figure this out, you may be ashamed you took so long. Once again it is about expectancy. Generally the sex of the doctor is unquestioned. Although this is supposed to be the age of women's rights, negative or absent expectancies still prevail and contribute toward counter productivity of attitudes. If you did not get the answer to this conundrum instantly, perhaps it says something about the nature of your expectancy. This is a very mild example but it is the mild ones we must watch because those are among the invisible cripplers of children. Of course we all have a expectancies of some sort otherwise we couldn't function efficiently throughout the day. They will be positive or negative. But we might as well keep a look-out so that where possible, for the good of ourselves and those around us, they are mostly positive.

It is important that your children have high levels of self-confidence. They won't if your expectancy of them (as distinct from their achievements) is low. There must be love and an acceptance of what they do, even if sometimes it's not what we had planned for them in terms of preferred careers. If they feel they have your backing and you are supporting them, they will shoot ahead. To do this we should drop the word 'children' from our minds and expectancies. Of course they are children, but there is no need to treat them as anything other than people, with the rights and dignity you would accord any other human being who walked into your house. Then will they succeed in the school world now, and in the adult world later.

Unless this backdrop to family values is present, successful problem-solving in the math arena will take a back seat because there are other problems that have to be addressed first.

POWER

How children feel about themselves feeds directly into math because math gives you power; the power to work things out, to have control over transactions, and to calculate outcomes, even if there are no numbers involved. Conversely, someone who has no problem-solving strategies feels powerless. In fact that's all that powerlessness is. Remember the old story of the Gingerbread Man? He demonstrated an early math skill when he said over and over, "I can do it, I can, I can, 'cos I'm the Gingerbread Man, I am."

You need three basic skills to get by. The first is how to write a letter, so you can apply for a job. The second is how to read your letter and the reply when it arrives. And the third is adequate math, so that when you go to the supermarket or buy a car you won't be ripped off. That's pretty much it. A school can teach those in about a year, if that.

The better you are at these three, the more personal control you feel. When you meet a child who is confident and knows they know about math, such a child is a joy to behold. She/he is bubbly, outgoing, fearless and sparkling, with a fierce brightness in the eyes and a sense of intellectual mischief.

Such a child has The Power. This person knows math is

easy, because it is reliable, predictable and available. When a child knows what to do, he/she can work anything out. That's all anyone is asking when it comes to math ability, not that the child learns screeds of knowledge and formulae and becomes a walking calculator, but that he has a confidence about being able to work something out, or know where to go to get the answer. It is important that he holds his head high and knows that if the answer is not immediately available there are ways to approach it when he becomes ready.

To have the skill of going somewhere to get the answer, the child must first have the confidence to move freely and approach all manner of people. When children feel powerful, they do well. In turn, parents feel good and successful about their own roles. The child makes the parent feel good and successful and that in turn comes back to the child.

There is an ancient Chinese saying that children are a mirror, and if you get pregnant then it is because you have a need to learn something about yourself. The potency of role modelling seems to make this statement accurate. Your self-esteem or lack of it will come back to reward or haunt you once you have children.

1. WATCH OUT, SOMEONE WANTS YOUR MIND

It's a sad fact of life that many parents don't seem to like themselves very much. We are taught to be unhappy, just as we are taught to feel unwell. You might say, oh that doesn't apply to me. But is there joy and laughter on your face as soon as you wake up in the morning? Do you leap out of bed in ecstasy at the thought of living another day? Does the huge grin on your face remain all day?

If you are like that you are very lucky, and unusual. That should be normal but we all know it's not. There are too many pressures on us, an iron heel of mortgages and responsibilities and bills grinding us down. We generally only get that feeling when we are on holiday, when those pressures are absent. If we could only get that feeling back into our daily existence, so that our children can then pick up on it, and use it for their own confidence!

We can only do it by deciding on a list of priorities, and acting on them. We can only do that when we make our lives into one big holiday. Years ago, my wife and I decided to leave the city behind and go and live on a house-bus so that our children would grow up in a stress-free environment, without the pressures of work and bills. We ended up doing it for ten years it was a huge adventure. It did what we imagined it would and our children blossomed. I'm not saying everyone has to go and buy a house-bus. That was just our way to made us feel valuable to ourselves. Seeing children grow up healthy and happy in turn works wonders on you.

We also are taught to feel unwell. From every corner of the media come stories of bad diets and the effects of eating wrong or not taking the right supplements. We are bombarded with grim stories of people being hospitalized. I have given up watching the six o'clock news, the very time that most of the country, myself included, likes to eat. The news is always full of accidents and I got sick of eating accidents. Surely a nation watching this stuff every single day it's going to become a nation of grim souls.

The rulers and controllers of our society want us in this powerless state because then the advertisers can show you products that claim to give you the joy and ecstasy missing from your life. They can sell you a fantasy about better times ahead. The advertisers run the TV networks.

It's also what the politicians want because they can promise you a better life if you vote for them next time. Never mind the fact that it was them that messed up the conditions today - they blame that on the last administration. Notice there is always money poured in for 'restructuring'. Don't they ever get it right? Also, a powerless nation is going to look more for strong leadership and be putty in the hands of whoever looks capable of fulfilling this role, whether or not that person is truly capable.

What's this got to do with math? Do you want your children to see you beaten down by the pressures and forces of society, in victim mode, and powerless to assert any energy that might help administer in reform; or would you rather they saw you as someone who was not going to be spiritually beaten by impossible odds, championing social causes that could make a difference?

If someone comes up to your child and tries to sell him drugs, will he have the forthrightness to repel them? Or will he run with the crowd, taking the line of least resistance because it's a quieter life? This is your turn to have a life. In the long run you have to be true to yourself. You have to be your own person. This requires work skills, life skills, and for the greater social good, a willingness to take risks; all skills part of personal power which are in the domain of math. Sooner or later you have to stand and be counted.

2. THE WORLD IS ACTUALLY YOURS

Look at the patterns of your living. Are you repeating the pattern your parents set for *themselves*? Has this pattern really got anything to do with you? What kind of a childhood did you have? Did you see a lot of your father? Are your children seeing more of you than you did of your father when you were growing up or about the same? Where did your present pattern come from?

Whatever you felt was unfair on you as you grew up should not be foisted onto your children. Otherwise your pain was not worthwhile. Only when you can see some worth in experiencing hardship can healing take place.

Math themes are central to all work habits. If you pursue private goals with vigor the math you require along the way will take care of itself. So too, will it be for your children. To isolate math as a pursuit separate from everything else is to set kids up for a fall. Math is the only subject where you can discuss with the child or class about solving problems; why doing thing one at a time is important, why mistakes are useful, and what questions and answers are really about. Math is the only subject where you can discuss life skills with children.

Some still have the weird notion that math is about arithmetic and sums. Math is no more only about numbers than life is; numbers are useful only insofar as they are tools to problem solving. As any high school pupil will yawn and tell you, algebraic letters are more universal now. As any computer programmer will tell you, there are only two numbers you need to know to rule the world, 1 and 0.

We need to show kids this broad scope of math. We need to discuss the mental role of the imagination and the emotional role of surprise, enabling math to come alive in a child's perception.

The problem is in part that schooling is confused with learning, grade advancement with education, a diploma with competence, and fluency with the ability to say something new. The imagination is only allowed to roam towards some previously determined successful outcome. The end result is a dead society run by dead thinking and stifling bureaucrats. Medical treatment is mistaken for health care, social work for the improvement of community life, police protection for safety, military poise for national security, and the rat race for productive work. Health, learning, and creativity are defined only in the areas we say they are going to appear in. We have institutionalized values and this has led to psychological impotence, killing real freedom, healthy self-discovery and self-direction. What is left is global misery, because that is the only free right that people are left with.

We have to take back the world - it belongs to *every*one in it. First we have to take back ourselves by recapturing our child-mind.

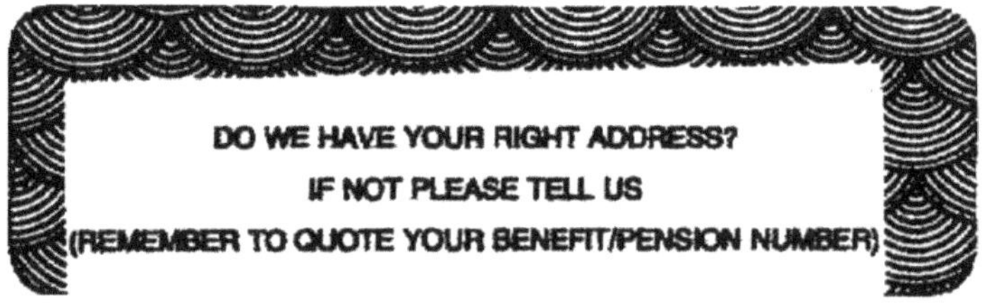

IS MY CHILD MATH-READY?

Why do you think 5 and 6 year olds write all over the page, don't plan their space and surprise themselves when they run out of room too quickly painting a picture? They are not being subversive or deliberately stupid - they have a limited concept of time and distance. If he/she is not aware of the limits of a page, then the top cupboard and the bottom cupboard in the kitchen is beyond her understanding too. So is 'on top of the bed' and 'under the bed'. Over and under are not just language but also early math concepts.

Although she may know these places as one-off situations, and she may have discovered with blocks that some on top of others make numerically more, she won't yet have the concepts of true top-ness and under-ness that can be transferred to symbolic universals, like what is 3 on top of 2.

Nor will she have the concept yet of abstraction, which is perceiving common quality, for instance when we see churches, houses and skyscrapers as 'buildings', cows, cats and dogs as 'animals', and in math, cartwheels, buttons and hula hoops as circles. Abstraction and proof were not even known to the Greeks, until they conquered the Balkan Peninsular and discovered some of these aspects of mathematical lore that had been accumulating for centuries.

Abstraction will not really be a formed concept until about the age of 8. I ask 5 to 7 year olds to find circles and triangles and squares on their clothes at the end of my shows, after we all make those shapes in the air to see if we know them. Even though they do that, by and large they still can't see them in the designs on their shirts etc. Although they can do triangles in the air with one finger, they don't see one inside a letter 'A'.

Adult concepts of space and time are not fully formed until 9 or 10 years. Educators refer to it as spatial awareness. Until the age of 9, things to do with geography (space) and history (time) are just stories. Yet teachers still talk about the Romans and the baby Jesus to very young children, who haven't an awareness of last week, let alone 2,000 years ago; and they do Children of Japan-type units, of people living across the sea, when these children don't know where the next street is, let alone another country.

For that reason too, it is at the 9 to 10 year age that team sports click in - to recognize a team is to appreciate yourself in time/space, and to fit in on that basis. Until that age children play largely by themselves in the company of others. After that age they actually play with others. That is why SHARE is such a difficult concept for young children. Many parents tear their hair trying, not realizing that the concept is foreign to the young mind; as foreign as walking is to a newborn baby.

It has also been noted that young children have far more trouble with 'before' than 'after', can handle 'more' but go to pieces over 'less'. In math, history is symbolically represented as 'before' on the number line, and the future is 'after'. And until the age of 9, when their perspective sense of what history is has not yet become a concept they can abstract, they won't have the feeling of it.

Children have trouble with 'early' for the same reason. Early/late is even more sophisticated than more/less and before/after. Early/late refers to an arbitrary and negotiable time-frame. "Come on!" Mum says, "or you'll be late for school!" But the child knows that it is still early in the day. In fact in the same day he may get up early, be late for school, be let out early, get home late, watch the early news and stay up late. "It's too early in your life to stay up late," grandmother may remind him kindly. Is this confusing? I'll say!

Check out understanding of these time-and-space frames before you expect the child to appreciate what actually happens in the processes of addition, subtraction, multiplication and division, which sometimes are introduced too quickly. Subtraction and division, which are about before and less, are the more difficult concepts to master. Most adults don't have fond memories of long division. And if you get lost driving around a strange city, even with a map, chances are that you never really perfected time/distance perception.

Many parents, perfectly naturally, are impatient for their children to succeed in the minimum time. But it is not the child's fault if he walks at 18 months and not 12 months. It is hardly something wilful if he is not well coordinated. Crawling and walking are acceptable biological maturational steps, but when kids don't want to retain things like their math facts and times tables, it is less unacceptable to parents and teachers bent on supplying a large agenda of useful information. The same goes for a seeming reluctance to remember what was explained barely five minutes ago. The immediate reaction is that the child is being deliberately uncooperative, especially if he has been displaying non-co-operation in other areas.

Yet mental maturation has to be just as valid as physical development. If a child was made to swim because an impatient adult thought he ought to learn and threw him in the deep end, he could well fear water all his life. If a child can't swim no-one says he has a swimming problem.

There are pleasant fun ways to introduce young children to water, showing them a variety of skills at their level, so that when they're ready they'll find themselves swimming despite themselves. For the rest of their days then, they stand more chance of enjoying it; and the choice is theirs whether they improve their skills or are just content knowing the basics. It is the same with learning math.

OOH YUK - SUBTRACTION AND DIVISION

Why does subtraction and division give children more headaches than addition and multiplication? It is because they are less natural to the child's mind. As a baby, he would have heard "more?" often said as the spoon came to the mouth. But mothers never say "Less? Less?" Also, children are taught to look forward to things. "Guess what? Next week we're going to visit Aunty Susan!" and not to look backward with the same enthusiasm. "Yesterday was your birthday!" doesn't quite have the excitement of "Tomorrow is your birthday!" Or, "in two years' time you're going to be seven!" is of more interest than "two years ago you were three."

What about multiplication versus division? As life itself multiplies and goes forward, division seems regressive. All life expands, plants grow up and out, and the child only has to watch mum's cooking to see that progression is positive and forwards along an imagined line, and not backward. You can't take a cake and reduce it to its ingredients any more than you can reduce and re-enter your mum's tummy.

I think that it has to be explained very carefully that division and subtraction are really quite hard concepts to work with; and although they are just adding the other way around, it's not a thing we do often. Like walking backwards, we have to watch our step more than when walking forwards, and we can't go nearly as fast.

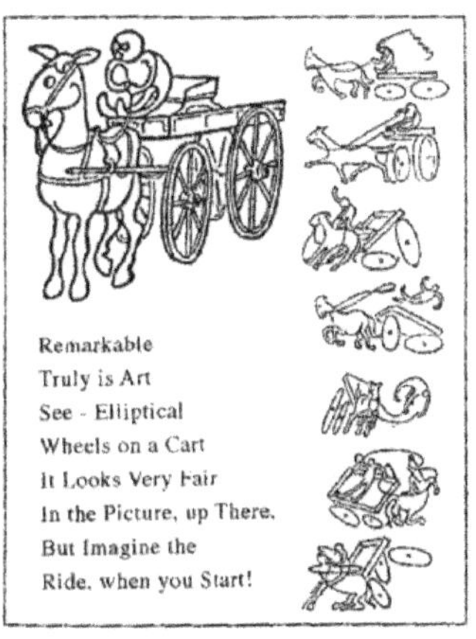

(- Gelette Burgess)

THE 4- TO 6-YEAR-OLD

At this age *your* input is crucial for healthy math attitudes. You can expect that children of this age range:

- are active and have lots of energy
- may be aggressive in their play
- can show extremes from being loud and aggressive to acting shy and dependent
- enjoy more group activities because they have longer attention spans
- like making faces and being silly
- may form cliques with friends and can be bossy
- may change friendships quickly
- may brag and engage in name-calling during play
- may experiment with swear words and bathroom words
- can be very imaginative and like to exaggerate
- have better control in running, jumping and hopping but tend to be clumsy
- are great talkers and questioners, and
- love to use words as rhymes, nonsense, and jokes

At this age they need to

- explore, experiment, investigate, and discover within limits
- use simple jigsaw puzzles
- practice outdoor play
- group items that are similar in size, shape, and color
- stretch their imaginations and curiosity
- talk a lot about numbers and use number concepts in daily routines, for example:
    1. Cooking - let's divide the cookie dough into two equal parts so we can bake some now and put the other half into the freezer
    2. Home projects - we're going to hang this picture 3 inches ABOVE the bookshelf in your room
    3. Home chores - how many plates do we need on the table? One for mum, one for dad, one for Jill. So how MANY'S that?
- talk about numbers that matter most to them - their age, address, phone number, height and weight.

3. MATH CONCEPTS FOR DISCUSSION:

Time (hours, days, months, years; older, younger, oldest, youngest, middle-sized, yesterday, today, tomorrow: "It's only 3 days until we go to Grandma's house. Let's put an X on the calendar so we won't forget."

Length (inches, feet, longer, taller, shorter, shortest): "This ribbon is too short to go around Grandma's present. Let's cut a longer ribbon, shall we?"

Weight (grams, pounds): "You already weigh 25lb. I can hardly lift such a big girl!"

Where you live (street number, phone): "These shiny numbers on our letter box are 51. We live at 51 on our street. When you go to play at Susan's, take this note with you. It's our phone number; 892-8745. Someday soon you'll know our phone number so you can call me if you need me."

Classifications (stacking or construction Lego-style blocks teach about color, shape, height, width, length, and depth)

Counting (Games that have scoring require children to count, for instance basketball, dice, dominoes)

It is best not to use chanting, drill exercises, worksheets, or flash card activities with children of this age range. These children can be turned off math if it doesn't fit in with the way they learn and play naturally.

Getting along (no materials required). Why is this a math concept? Learning to get along with others teaches him to get along with himself. If he has a frustration during play, he will be more calm and more strategic and employ problem-solving skills more effectively. Children who are kind, helpful, patient and loving, generally do better in school.

4. *WHAT TO DO:*

Let your child know that you are glad to be his parent. Give him personal attention and encouragement. Set aside time when you and your child can do fun things together. Encourage your spouse, or an adult member of the opposite sex to do the same. your happy feelings toward your child will help him feel good about himself.

Set a good example. Show your child what it means to get along with others and to be respectful. Say please and thank you. Treat people in ways that show you care what happens to them. Ask for things in a friendly way. Help your child to find ways to solve conflicts with others. Help him figure out what will happen if he tries to settle his angry feelings by hitting a playmate. "Johnny, I know that James took your truck. But if you hit James and you have a big fight, then James will have to go home and you won't be able to play anymore today. What's another way that you can tell James that you want the truck back?"

Johnny tells James he's upset and wants it back. He lets James play with it for another 5 minutes, meanwhile playing with something else which James may be more interested in. Listen to your children's problems. Sometimes that is all they need for them to solve their own problems.

Oh by the way... according to my teachers I'm suffering from a lack of discipline in the house... See to it, will you?

They don't have to work out everything on their own, help is available. Be physically affectionate. Children need hugs, kisses, an arm over the shoulder, walking holding hands, and a pat on the back. This tells your child you love them. Say it too. Don't assume that because you are loving parents your actions will speak for themselves. Teach your child the international hand sign for "I love you." Or a secret sign worked out between the two of you. You can 'sign' each other as he leaves home and goes to school.

Children need social skills. Teachers and other children will enjoy his company if he gets along with others. If he feels included and popular he will not develop learning blocks. But if he marginalizes himself through his temper outbursts, his academic progress will suffer.

WHAT IS THIS NUMBER LINE?

How do you count? Is it up to 100, or *along* to it. Do you think of it getting fatter from the middle? Children may have a different perspective on counting to that of their parents. When mum says count up to 6 it may be confusing to a child who thinks that 6 is not *up* in the sense of higher, because that has not been in her experience. Six may even be down to her, because she found that five blocks don't fall down but six do. After all, if you throw a ball a few feet up it also comes a few feet down.

We should be careful we don't prejudice our children's reality. Once when doing a show, I asked a 5 year old what she could count up to. Her immediate reaction was to look up at the ceiling, not saying a word. I realized she didn't know what I was talking about. Since then I have never said 'count up' to a child, just in case that child didn't. Instead I say, "how far can you count", or "how many numbers do you know", or "what can you count to."

Most children think of numbers in terms of age. If 5-year-old Amanda has an older brother Brian who is 7, she will have the sense that 7 is higher because Brian is taller. But what if Brian was a paraplegic? More is not always higher, or even bigger. 96 peanuts is not bigger than one house. That is why it is important to seek out the child's perspective first, and then take things from her starting line.

I once had another child on stage, whose name was Emma. She, too, was five. I said, "Can you count?" and she immediately obliged, "zero, one, two, three, four, five, six, seven, eight, nine, ten, eleven..." she would have gone on but I put my hand on her shoulder and stopped her, commenting "That's GREAT. Thank you. You count well!" whereupon a little friend of hers in the front row shouted out "NO - SHE HASN'T FINISHED YET!" ("Oh yes she *has*," I replied)
When it comes to sequence, which is away from a starting line, there are 4 basic types in elementary math. We call it the number line and it could look like this, (but it could equally be vertical):

1 2 3 4 5 6 7 8 9 10 11 12 13 14 15 16 17 18 19 20

ADDITION is forward movement along this line.
SUBTRACTION is a reverse movement.
MULTIPLICATION is a faster forward movement.
DIVISION is a faster reverse movement.

5. ABOUT MULTIPLYING

Basically multiplying is just a fast way of counting. But it is something different to just fast adding. After all, when you run you use different muscles to when you walk. Sometimes you walk, as in a library, and sometimes it's appropriate to run as in a race. It is not a good idea to run in a library or walk in a race. It's the same with adding and multiplying - adding goes slowly just accumulating one extra amount in each operation. but multiplying means things arrive faster, as in whole numbers, or *go* faster as in multiplying fractions.

For thousands of years multiplying was not as we do it. The ancient method of computing numbers of bricks in a wall or tiles on the floor was by counting each one. It was time-consuming. About 500 years ago, the Multiplication Table came into being, and was part of every artisan's tool-kit. The answers were engraved and etched onto wood or metal and carted around much like calculators are today. Committing times tables to memory is a relatively new idea. It would have astonished the early men of mathematics that small children would one day be required to commit the whole table to memory.

Of course there is no need. The Greeks and Romans got by without learning their tables. They achieved math understanding by moving pebbles in grooves like the abacus, and by using equipment like protractors, compasses, knots at equal intervals on lengths of rope, and various other crude counting systems..

It is now known that only 30% of the population respond well to rote learning, which means learning things by heart e.g. times tables. This means that in any classroom in any school, 70% of the WHOLE class are turning off and tuning out when they are asked to learn parrot fashion something that they don't actually understand. This is not good enough by today's standards, and rote learning is on the way out. It had its origins with the earliest schools which were run by the monks. Back then, everything was chanted, like Greek and Latin verses and passages of the bible.

However I still go into schools and hear the chanting of

times tables. Suppose you were told to learn the lyrics of 12 different songs, all to the tune of Amazing Grace. You would probably get confused. That would be the worst way to learn something. Yet that is what happens when a child is required to commit times tables to memory.

I am not saying don't learn them. But there are better ways. For the proof of the pudding, ask a group of adults to do a tables test and the chances are some will get some wrong, even after years of being taught them and committing them to memory.

In Britain an experiment was done whereby one group of children were given tables to learn by heart and the other group were given NO instruction, but calculators to recreationally fool around with. At the end of a set period (about 3 months) the groups were tested for their knowledge of times tables. The group that were given the traditional instruction method failed miserably. Those who had been playing with calculators knew far more because the information had come to them in a stress-free way. *Oh yes, six eights - I think I saw that yesterday - um - 48?* From this and other such research has come much in the way of changes to the curricula, which now includes supplying calculators to five year olds.

If you ask any child to recite a TV ad she will sing for you the jingle which is her current favorite. She won't have ever sat down and learned it word for word or written it out and recited over and over, or been given it for homework and been tested for it from a little notebook list. So how come she knows this piece of relatively meaningless drivel so well?

Why can't she remember *useful* things with the same potency?

The fault is in the teaching, not the child. We all learn best peripherally. When information comes in from the side, so to speak, it *is* stress-free - there is no-one standing over your shoulder demanding that you learn it, and no-one going to test you the next day. Such information, if it is accessed regularly, is much more likely to remain in the brain for longer periods. Think of all the things you remember from your childhood - What percentage of those memories were you MADE to learn at school and how many do you remember anyway even though they weren't part of the school experience?.

What you will remember will have some emotional hook to it. You could have been excited, scared, lonely or angry at the time. It is the association of positive emotions that makes for successful retention.

I can still remember Sally Richardson making a rude noise during religious instruction. I was about 8 and the whole episode still burns in my mind. Why do I remember that? Because it was so exciting. The teacher was severely angry, and that was *always* fun. Added to the delight was that everyone was glad it wasn't them that did it. And we all were eager to see what the teacher would do. Sally got away with it. I bet everyone in that class still remembers that incident as strongly as I do; nearly half a century later. If only I could have remembered schoolwork as well.

It is possible to inject excitement into multiplication. Imagine the difference between a teacher chalking 15 X 15 = 225 on the blackboard, and that same teacher taking a spray can and SPRAYING that same message all along a newly painted wall or along the precious side of the school. Or on the door of the principal's office. *While he was inside!* Can you imagine it? The effect would be electric. Those who witnessed such a subversive act would indeed know what fifteen fifteens were 'til their dying day.

I'm not advocating lawlessness, but bizarreness, strangeness, surprise and excitement - yes. Dream up wild ways to present things, even if it means dressing up, making queer noises, or creating mess. (It could be a set-up, with the principal in on it, and washable paint). Why not have a wall especially put aside for spraying math or spelling messages onto. You could even put a convicted tagger in charge of its upkeep!

6. ABOUT USING FOOD

One good idea is, if you want an interesting way of doing ANY math use food. Kids respond to food much more than beads, and small counters, blocks and rods.

Lay out some pebbles (or peanuts or raisins) in a row, say, 12. Say: "If you can do this well you can eat the result at the very end. Put your finger next to any number. Which is it? Good. Now I'm going to get you to go 1 more. Tell me what number your finger is at now. Now another 2 more. What number's that? One more again. What number are you on now?"

"Now, you start off this time on this number we just got to. Go 1 the other way. What number now? Go 2 that way if you can."

"Now we'll start at the beginning of the line. Put your finger next to number 1. Jump 2 spaces along. Good. You're now at number? 3! Right."

"Put your finger on number 1, now 2, now 3. Okay, TAKE AWAY 2. How many have you got? How many are left? Taking away is the same as moving your finger which way, left or right?"

"Put the two back so there are 3 again. Putting 2 back is the same as going how many along?"

"Start with the complete line, and on 0. Move the finger in big jumps, up to 3 then hop over another three to 6 and then to 9. Did my finger go along any faster? When we move up in sets of 3, we move how many at a time? 3! Good! That's why we say we move one, 3 times. Also, we moved three all at once. So let's move 4 three times and see what number we come to."

Talking, talking, talking, that's the secret. Looking at it from all angles and taking the child's ideas, too.

7. ABOUT MENTAL ARITHMETIC.

You're not mental if you can't do mental. Math is as much about the operator as the operation You learn about your own curiosity, your own mistake-making, your own confidence in risk-taking, your own potential for ideas, and about changing your own mind when appropriate. These come from the math experience - measuring the world, and playing with its possibilities. The units of measurement are arbitrary; they will vary with the exercise: The real math is in the act of measuring.

Arithmetic is the old word for the computational area of math. This word has now been replaced by 'algorithms' and 'problem-solving'. Over the years, due to laxity and indifference, educators have allowed the word math to mean arithmetic, so those who had trouble computing came to think that math is beyond them. But much math hardly looks at arithmetic - geometry, algebra, topology, calculus, computer science, logic - these have their own rules. This is not to say that arithmetic has no place.

Professor of Mathematics Ian Stewart of Warwick University says our minds aren't geared to doing arithmetic. There are psychological studies that show humans aren't digital - our brains don't handle numbers digitally as computers do. For arithmetic, which is still important in the modern world, we have to divert the natural talents of the brain and make it work more precisely than it was evolved to.

"I think the world's leading mathematicians are probably very bad at arithmetic. They have a feel for the whole of the problem, like a concert musician who doesn't have to think about how to play each note because he or she is concentrating on the overall performance. At school however, the emphasis is on making sure that you can play each note correctly, that you get the right answer. The trouble is, after three of four hours of doing that, a child is too tired for the really interesting sorts of math that they could handle." Arithmetic has used numerals to express ideas and to depict a relatively small number of processes, which can be mastered quickly but which very soon become boring and pointless if they are ends in themselves.

Whatever you do should be for a perceivable reason: if the reason can't be perceived you should be making enquiries to that end - only then will children know value and their own truth. The child should not feel he's being worked like a donkey for the sake of it. Veteran work donkeys don't end up more intelligent or any better off than young fresh ones - just more tired, that's all.

The point to much math is the sheer game of it in a personal or social sense; how it can unite a group in a joint exercise or enable a parent and child to have some fun.

When parents pull their child out of school because the child is not coping; generally it is because he is not coping with math - which generally means mental arithmetic. Those who struggle over it often feel there is something wrong with their brain. In the classroom no format exists for questioning the system. Nowhere is the concept "curriculum disability" heard.

As the mind was not designed to do arithmetic, it was certainly not designed to do mental arithmetic. We have a tool for that, called a calculator. In the same way, one finger was never designed to bore a hole in wood: we have a tool for that called a drill. Again as the human hand is designed to go and get the drill and hold it so the hole can be bored, the head's function is to decide to use the calculator.

Calculators make all conventional arithmetic up to a 14-year old's level obsolete. Yet children are still denied the use of them in many schools. The feeling is that understanding goes by the wayside. This is a valid point, but can be overcome in other ways. Calculators are part of essential technology, like drills, and are here to stay. Schools must embrace them and set about teaching understanding using new skills like guesstimating.

The day is coming when children will not be required to memorize things by heart. Sitting next to each other they will be encouraged to talk and share ideas. In tests they may even be encouraged to cheat. When that day comes, children will enjoy school. The biggest hurdle will be to sell the idea to parents, who don't realize the way the world of education has been changed by research into learning. They still think that the way they were taught should prevail today. Children were only bored then with meaningless exercises - today they set fire to schools.

"Now, sir, you say the vandals got in last night and wrecked the classrooms but no-one noticed until 11:45 this morning."

8. USING "BETCHA"

The language of children is different to that of adults. It is a language of opposites, of seeing everything as a challenge, pitting themselves against these challenges and against each other in those challenges. Oh, I betcha can't do this, I betcha YOUR dad can't run faster than MY dad.

This language drives adults mad very quickly. However, it is how children learn and it explains why they learn well from each other - because they speak the same language and they understand each other.

Adults can use this language too, and if you do your child will love you for it. It is not patronizing, but shows your child how much you are prepared to have fun with him. Basically it's like forbidding a child to wash. Washing then becomes the only thing he wants to do. At any time of the day or night I used to say to my 4 year old:

"I betcha can't tell me what 2 sixes are."

"Yes, I'm going to!"

"Oh please don't!"

"I will, ha-ha!"

"No, no…"

"Yes, um ..twe.."

"NO NO..!" (Mock hiding head in hands)

"TWELVE!"

"Oh, NO! Alright, just so long as you don't tell me 3 fours. NO ONE can work that out!"

"I can!"

"Betcha can't."

"TWELVE!"

This approach does get them going. It's classic clowning technique and I used to use it for spelling also:

"I betcha you can't spell 'machinery'."

"I bet I CAN. I'm going to ask Mum right NOW!"

Some call it negative psychology. Others will call it nauseous stupidity. I think it's a very powerful tool, and not at all negative. You have to carry the act off with conviction, as if you really do not believe they can do whatever it is you are suggesting. Kids love to think they know more than you, the big person. If they can seize a chance at pointing out your ineptness they will. Also they love to see a great big person in trouble, and if you appear to have difficulty doing something they know they can do without much effort, they'll spring into mental (or physical) action. (Aha, just what you want!)

9. FOR OLDER KIDS

1) Say "Betcha that if you open up a phone book to any page and mark off twenty successive numbers(numbers in a row), out of those twenty numbers there will be at least two phone numbers that have the same last two digits(for example, 4216 and 8316)." At first glance this seems impossible. There are 100 possible combinations for those last two digits (from 00 to 99). Mathematically, however, the odds are 7 to 1 in your favor. In other words, every 100 times you play this, you will only lose 13 times.

2) Say "After doing the last one, I'm going to give you a chance to WIN. Open the phone book and mark off the last two digits of any number. Count down forty-five numbers, and I'll betcha that those two numbers that you marked off

won't appear as the last two digits of any of those forty-five numbers. Don't forget, you're getting nearly twice as many numbers to work with as I had a just a minute ago. Odds: 3 to 2 in your favor. Out of every 100 times, you will win 60 times.

3) Here's a good betcha for a group of about 40 people. Say to the group "I betcha there are at least two people here with the same birthday." Chance of success is 8 to 1 to you. Out of every 100 times, you will be correct 87 times. With 50 people in the room the probability becomes 99.8% that there will be matching birthdates. Just ask anyone at random for the first one.

MATH BY CHOCOLATE

Using a chocolate bar that costs a dollar or two, you can create a hugely exciting math lesson, taking the number line into a new dimension that will have your little Johnny foaming at the mouth.

The multiplication table resembles a chocolate bar. You have to adapt your program according to the size of your bar. Most bars come in a 6 X 10 King Size, a 5 X 8 tablet, or a 7 X 1. Let's work first with the King Size (any flavor!)

Multiplication Table

1	2	3	4	5	6	7	8	9	10
2	4	6	8	10	12	14	16	18	20
3	6	9	12	15	18	21	24	27	30
4	8	12	16	20	24	28	32	36	40
5	10	15	20	25	30	35	40	45	50
6	12	18	24	30	36	42	48	54	60
7	14	21	28	35	42	49	56	63	70
8	16	24	32	40	48	56	64	72	80
9	18	27	36	45	54	63	72	81	90
10	20	30	40	50	60	70	80	90	100

1. Write out the table opposite first, on a piece of stiff card
2. Find out what times table needs working on.
3. Break the bar accordingly.

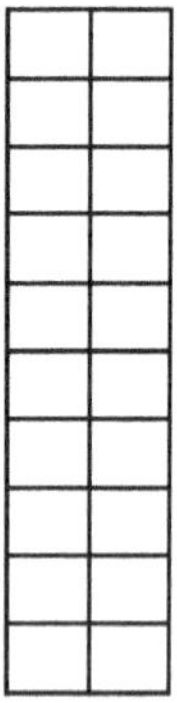

If he needs work on the two times, break it like this two bar, as pictured.

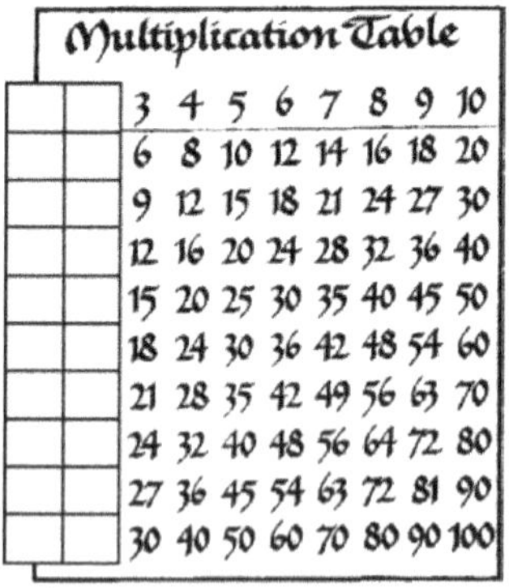

Multiplication Table

3	4	5	6	7	8	9	10
6	8	10	12	14	16	18	20
9	12	15	18	21	24	27	30
12	16	20	24	28	32	36	40
15	20	25	30	35	40	45	50
18	24	30	36	42	48	54	60
21	28	35	42	49	56	63	70
24	32	40	48	56	64	72	80
27	36	45	54	63	72	81	90
30	40	50	60	70	80	90	100

Now just overlay the two bar on the table and talk about it from all angles and points of discussion. For instance, we have a bar that is a pile of two's. How many twos? Let's count them: 20. We put a 20 over this lot, there, 20 are covered. What happens when we get another 20 just like this and put it next to it - how many will both cover? - 40! What if we broke this 20 up into ten little lots of two tablets each - let's see what they will cover and what stories we can come up with.

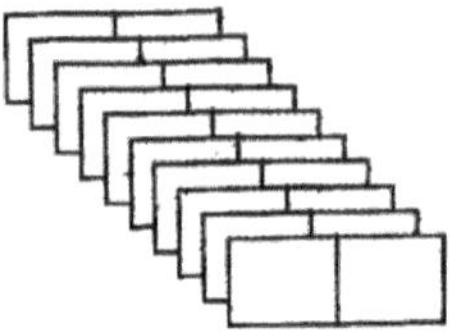

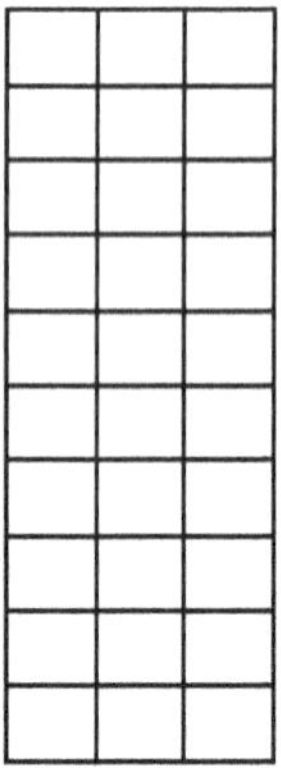

Now you can do the same with lots of three and four. Starting off with the big blocks and breaking them down can be the child's job! And he can eat the bits that fall off the side every time he breaks them.

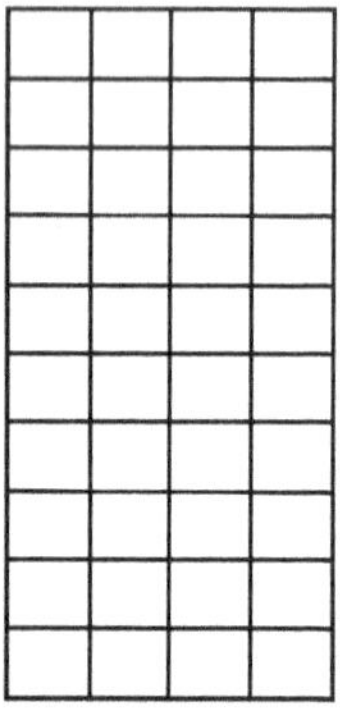

You can do division, addition, subtraction, fractions, and simple shapes with these blocks. Talk about what happens when... Get him to predict before you do it, and then check his answer. A few loose ones will be useful too. These can be superimposed on top of the others to create a high pile. You will find that you invent your own games and ways of explaining different systems. Mostly, he will just enjoy touching the chocolate and dreaming about eating it. What's wrong with that? Imagine if he said he was dreaming of touching the math equipment!

Make sure everyone washes their hands first. Alternatively, decree it that no-one touches the chocolate until eating time comes. Until then the pieces have to be moved around with a knife blade or salad tweezers.

Don't forget that math *understanding* is your aim. The Multiplication Table means nothing of itself, until you start moving ones and twos around on it and they can see how numbers start to stack up.

Ask him to test *you*. Kids love doing that. Tell him that you are having trouble with your 7 times table, and would he mind asking you some questions about it just to get your mind working. Give him a check list of the answers so he can refer to them, as well as a seven block of tablets to move around on the multiplication table initially, and then seven single ones to use when the seven block doesn't fit.

Pretend to stumble and hesitate and then give a wrong answer so he can correct you. This way he is learning it as well, only he doesn't know it.

MATH AS A SECOND LANGUAGE

In the shortened form of mathematics there is one other word that ends in '-ath and that is bath, which is an agreed turn-off word amongst children. Perhaps there is a discomfort saying math. If you think this is a factor with your child, then get him/her to call it something else. But children can handle strange words. Look at dehumidifier, videocassette, supercalifragilisticexpialidocious. There's a popcorn product in Australia called lollygobbleblissbombs which kids love and all seem happy to say. And what about Teenage Mutant Ninja Turtles. But the word has to relate to something they can get their hands on, their fingers into, or twist their mind around in their imagination. There has to be something cute about it for this to happen. Unless it's about food. Then they'll remember anything.

If we are not making it cute for them we can all go and blame the word. And if you think it helps to delete it I think you should. We want them to recognize and be able to manipulate math so it can be useful in their lives and many of us happily do great heaps of math every day without calling it anything.

Kids first meet The Word when they're told in first grade to 'get out the Math Equipment'. It's still just blocks and counting beads to them and in some schools it seems like an activity whereby you make a mess to music. The mess is because you end up with little bits all over the place, and the music is because you do counting chants.

It is very hard to shield kids from what unthinking adults say about math. Around school age they start really listening to what is said at home when math gets mentioned. Somebody even visiting the family only has to drop how they were no good at math, believing they are getting onside with the child. Gleeful stories of scrapes with cruel math masters emerge. Even if the child did like it before, he might now start to look for reasons to dislike it because there are better stories to be had from math-suffering. And we all do things for the stories, we dine out on them.

Sometimes parents say it's hard but necessary. Or, you need it later in life. They say the same about reading. My grandmother lived a happy and productive life without learning to read. Granted though, your job opportunities will be limited. But in some ways she was better off. When you can read, you have to! It is impossible to look at a word and not read it. So the advertisers have control over you immediately whilst those who can't read are left alone. To most reading is regarded as a right, a joy, and a necessity. But if a child experiences extreme difficulty, it could be that either reading is not his/her thing at the moment, or that the best teaching style hasn't been found.

There is no such thing as a lazy child. He is either sick or misguided. If he is sick take him to the doctor. If he is misguided guide him better or find him a better guide. If you have lost your way it could be that you have been given a faulty map.

I wish people would stop telling their children that life itself is hard but necessary. It is a travesty that children might learn not to enjoy things.

When they pull out the math equipment, and they like playing with it, I suggest *sometimes* calling it math, because for some kids who already are forming a strangeness over the word, they could be put off. We could call it The Games Box, or The Fun Cupboard. They want to talk about what can happen and possible results of their interaction with it. They don't really care what it's called. To get bogged down with abstract symbolism before the child is ready is recipe for confusion.

English is now so complex and so full of alternatives that many sub-languages are being de-emphasized to make them more user-friendly. You see it happening with for example, legalese, scientific writing, technical instruction manuals and medicine. For example, there is more willingness to drop 'tonsillitis' and say 'sore throat', swap 'lumbago' for 'back pain', and 'accessorize your ensemble' is back to 'do you want a brooch with that dress?'

There is no reason why words like Add, Plus, Minus, and Multiply need be thrown at young children, especially when they are not words likely to be used elsewhere by them in their play environment just yet and before they are aware of different processes. For 'minus', children use drop, pinch, lose, forget, and take away. They are always dropping, losing, and forgetting things, and having things taken away. Same with plus. Kids say stack, squash, sit-on-top-of, and the most commonly heard; put, as in put it there, put one here. A simple 'and' would do for plus. It is often forgotten that simple everyday words are already represented with math symbols. For example:

of.......x
and.......+
more.......>
is, are.......=
the, a, that, this, thing, it.......1
not, none, nothing, no more, gone.......0
is not......=/=
both.......2
few.........3
what?......algebraic x
where?.......(   )brackets
gone, owe.......-1
pieces.......fraction bar line
a bit.......decimal point

No-one is suggesting the words of math be thrown out. Rather, in the early years, let the unfamiliar terms seep in gradually and in their own time they will come to be used more often.

Consider 2 times 3. People don't say that in everyday conversation. However they do say what it really means, which is 3 two times, in other words, if we're using sticks, 2 groups of three.

111   111

We might say 'I saw three birds two times this morning' and this is acceptable. We don't say "I saw 2 times 3 birds sitting in the tree". Literally we should really be writing three two times as 32X. Of course we can't, because that would also read *thirty-two times*, which would mean something else. So we write three two times as two times three 2 X 3.

I suggest that this is confusing to adults, let alone to children. I know from experience that small children can get upset by this and don't even have a way of asking to clear it up. Teacher's don't check all this out. They just expect a kid to look at 2 X 3 and understand that it is three two times.

Similarly when we say 2 X 3 = 3 X 2 and tell children to learn it. Some children won't agree with this so-called Law. They know seeing two birds three times in one morning is not the same as seeing three birds twice. And one side, 2 X 3, is back-to-front compared with the other, 3 X 2. Also they sound different when read out. The teacher says both equal 6. Yes but that's only *one* similarity. They're both written too, on the same page, on the same day, and both of equal length, but that still doesn't necessarily make them the same.

What about 1 + 0 = 0 + 1? It doesn't necessarily mean the same thing. If you don't put an extension on a building; is this the same as having nothing and building something? You must carefully explain what you really mean to a child. That will help him to be precise in his answer too. And that's what math is, an attempt at precision. At school I got into trouble when the teacher asked us, what side of the road do cars drive on in NZ? I didn't understand the question. I said both.

Symbols are helpful to the scientist because they serve to shortcut his thinking. But to many lay people symbols make mathematics not a universal language of philosophy but a massive linguistic barrier between the scientists and the humanists.

It's confusing introducing the language for math, one that they don't use in the playground, without explaining it first. It would be far easier if all kids spoke ancient Greek, but they don't.

Only part of the vocabulary of mathematics has been grabbed by science. Most of it - and all the grammar - remains in the sphere of general human thought and everyday activity and interaction. Mathematics has as more to do with philosophy, economics, cooking, musical composition, crowd control, art and ball games than it has to do with physics.

WHY TEACHERS FAIL

As a show opener I ask audiences, "So t ell me honestly, who doesn't like math?" I am being light-hearted, and usually get about a 90% response in the show of hands. In one school recently, two teachers also put up their hands. They were serious and I inwardly groaned - it was a pity that the children saw that.

In this country, 80% of all teachers do not take math beyond the fifth form. We can reasonably conclude that 80% of all teachers don't like math, or at school they would have taken it further. These are the people entrusted to making math palatable to young minds.

Specialization should be occurring in primary school, so that the person who liked teaching math should do it all; the person who liked music should do it all, etc. Then you would get enthusiastic teaching staff, who repeated successful programs.

The parent who thinks she hates math can do no harm just in mentioning math words around the home; 'long' and 'short' for toddlers, and words about shapes etc. for older children. In time and effort it costs very little, and you have to talk anyway to your kids. You might as well stick in the occasional educative word.

Then when the children start school they would not find the language of math so unusual. It would be Oh *those* words! Mum uses THEM all the time. It could be part of the natural day, for both environments.

Someone with a negative teaching attitude will unavoidably be imparting that negative attitude to the audience, through body language, impatience, lack of creativity and spontaneity, and general lack of interest in pupils' queries.

One or two schools might tell you, oh but we have to do it this way, or that feel so tied to the curriculum, if they veered they could lose their teaching job. Does job protection loom higher than the esteem and well-being of the pupils. (Hmm.. a resounding yes) If you believe in the children's rights and their rights to a healthy confidence then perhaps it *is* up to you to fight to save their souls from the possible destructive intentions of an impersonal school system.

Most staff will assure you they are not being destructive, and throw up their hands in horror at this suggestion. But any channeling of children into a format, a sameness, (which is not to say routines are not beneficial, but children will come up with their own) confuses process with substance. A new logic is assumed, which can stifle a newly emerging inquisitive mind.

When the child enters school at the age of five or thereabouts, there is a fire in the eyes, they believe they are going to learn magic. In a year that look is often largely gone, in two years of schooling, may be completely gone. Teachers will confirm this but won't see it as a problem, don't know what to do about it, or don't even think that the situation is preventable. "That's just the way things are," is the general retort. That's what the Nazis said to the Jews. Where will reform come from? Will it only come when enough parents have pulled children from schools and into home-schooling? Your child only has one childhood, one chance to form mentally safe attitudes to life and learning and loving. Knowing a bad situation exists whereby his school is not catering for him, because he is an exploring child but something is turning him off math, is it not your duty to keep his magic alive?

Many students, especially those who are poor, *intuitively* know what the schools don't do for them. Where before the call was for more education and health funding, now the perception is that more funding is just perpetuating already-flawed systems.

Perhaps at this stage we should examine what being a teacher is all about. What the word teacher means and entails is quite different today to what the same word meant thirty something years ago.

TEACHING IS HARMFUL TO CHILDREN

Teaching is far more than injecting knowledge into others. A student isn't simply a sponge ready to absorb knowledge. No-one can put an idea into another person's mind. A student must want to learn in order for the teacher's presentation of material to be grasped.

Children learn by discovery, not by being taught. The notion of "I did it myself mummy" is still the main spur in all of us, whether we are 4 year olds in a sandpit or 40 year olds in business. The way to get anyone agitated and motivated has always been to tell them that they can't do something. We have wonderful stories of young crippled athletes who overcame impossible odds to eventually win Olympic gold.. If you do not allow a child self-discovery, you create a dependence and insecurity. This produces the adult lacking in confidence who will always need to be told what to do.

I once helped out at a day care center. At 11.0 each morning everyone had to have 'Freedom Time.' It was compulsory, whether or not each child was in the mood; it was programmed, and it was finite. It was resented, too, by everyone except the supervisor.

Freedom is not something you can program, any more than you can go up to a comedian and ask him to say something funny. The price of freedom is eternal vigilance. We must be on guard that our spontaneity is not robbed from us by administrators whose interests are power and control.

If YOU draw it for me...
If YOU paint it for me...
If YOU cut it out for me...

...All I learn is that YOU can do it better than ME.

If a child is interested he will learn by himself; he won't have to be instructed. If he is not interested, he will not be receptive. In either case, the learning happens because of *his* energy and the contribution of himself to the situation, not because there was a teacher doing it. Teacher might well have been there and necessary, but the child taught himself.

By attending to an achievement rate, teaching attends to a failure rate too. Because children are so anxious to please, the more sensitive of them come unstuck when they cannot fulfil unreasonable mental demands, and because the unwanted focusing upon failure consumes their effort to succeed.

Recent good trends in teaching have been towards creating inquiry environments, where the teacher's role is as facilitator. In an ideal inquiry environment, students raise and then answer their own questions and rediscover the subject matter. For this to work one requires a classroom with one

teacher per pupil, or at least one teacher per small group so that all get an equal chance to contribute often. Otherwise, while the group is waiting for the teacher to arrive from the previous group, they lose interest and become disruptive.

Although recommended and fine in principle, this often underfunded idea is unworkable. Also it requires the participation of each pupil's inquisitive nature. We can't always count on students wanting to learn and to ask the right questions at the same or an allotted time. Once again we are advocating 'freedom time' when *we* decide.

So it would be preferable to encourage the formation of those questions in student's minds at any time of the school or non-school day, and for the expression of those ideas and the provision for them to bear fruit.. A good teacher does this by ENTERTAINING students. It may be that the teacher entertains with interesting material that the students don't want to put down. Or it may be that the teacher acts as a performer in an attempt to make any material interesting. If we can mix elements of both, we can accomplish our goal of keeping students interested in, and thinking about their work. A 'performance' to start things off can act as a catalyst to get questions flowing, but what is performed should hold the main messages of what is to be learned.

Many teachers feel that teachers are not there to entertain

and that learning should carry its own reward. That's not how the world is. People should be kind to each other so there is no need for wars and no-one should be greedy or go hungry. Sadly everyone doesn't think like that at once. Cultural and religious conflicts are carried forward into succeeding generations, and when it comes to greed, some people's imagined needs are greater than others. By the same argument teaching-classrooms won't work for everyone. But places of entertainment will.

If you turn on the TV you will see that entertainers rule. Presidents are selected because of their looks (Kennedy), their voice or hair (Clinton), their record in Hollywood (Reagan), their athletic achievements (Gerald Ford), or other spotlight experiences like military victory (Eisenhower). Sportspeople are asked their opinions about things they know nothing about, otherwise the industry of endorsement advertising would not work. Today's leaders, sporting heroes, and even some eminent scientists are in fact our entertainers.

Our teachers *must* entertain. The teachers of today even inherit a performing theatre as their workplace, where there is one person in front of many. But teaching is less than ideal from a performing point of view.. Most professional performers rely on a compere to get the audience in the mood for them to them appear.. One does not walk onto a stage cold from the street and immediately start acting like teachers do at the start of the day. Techniques of voice projection, posture and movement have to be learned so that an audience is warmed up, before any performance can begin, so they don't turn off early. Exactly the same dynamics and requirements apply to acting or teaching.

Unfortunately what they teach in teachers' colleges has little to do with the how-tos. They should get magicians or clowns in, because those two types of entertainer know about audience psychology. A magician makes a crucial move when the audience is least paying attention - there are two main times - when they are laughing or gasping in surprise at the previous routine. For this to happen the performer must be totally aware of how and when to guide the audience's reactions. A clown makes his move when the audience is most paying attention - often to something else. They don't teach this at teacher's colleges but they thoroughly teach it at magic and clowning courses.

Whereas the magician retains power and presents an air of mystery which builds tension and excitement, the clown gives power away so that his audience think they know more than him. Both styles alternate in teaching, because power is being transferred. The nature of power is that, like alternating current, it should go both ways. Then each party is enriched and the teaching experience becomes a shared event.

Others who know the science of performing are actors, orators, stand-up comics, singers, politicians, and masters of ceremony. In their own way they are all teachers because they take command and people are willing to follow their leadership.

When I speak of teaching, I also mean parenting. Parents are the first and only true teachers. A regular school teacher is a substitute parent, and it was written as such into the teachers' conduct book of rules (in NZ called the Teachers' Legal Handbook). That was, until a few years ago, when the Education Board deleted the relevant phrase without telling anyone.

The actual words were that the role of the teacher was 'in loco parentis' which means in place of the parent. By removing this phrase the policy makers thought they might release teachers from accountability. It is a shame that teachers are ever held accountable, because parents really have the responsibility for shaping attitudes. Teachers would do better to push for less accountability and more *loco parentis* . After all, you don't blame the babysitter if the children turn out to be delinquent.

Whether we like it or not, teaching has to be about entertaining. And entertainment is about selling.

THE SELL

Once, selling was about making people feel good *when* they bought a product. That is still part of it - of course you don't want buyers feeling bad. These days there is a different emphasis. Advertising psychology has grown up as a science. Nowadays it dictates that you want them to feel good *first, so that* they'll buy the product. There's a difference. The latter approach forms a more lasting bond with the salesperson which could lead to more sales.

We all like being praised. If a salesman can make a buyer feel good about herself, she will look forward to the salesman's company in the hope of hearing nice things said. And one sure way to be in the salesman's company is to buy his products. This is bound to please the salesman who in turn will probably say more nice things.

Selling is about motivation and empowering. Like the man who liked the blades so much he bought the company. To sell effectively the seller must himself be empowered and motivated. He must first have thoroughly sold the product to himself. Salespeople are forever attending inspiration and motivation courses, to keep up that charged sales energy. It keeps them alive, and well, and feeling great! You may well ponder why no-one tells school administrators about these findings.

True, there's money at the end of it. Some salesmen, failing to reach their projected sales quota, lose their motivation and personal esteem. Maybe these people were not cut out to be in sales in the first place. Their motivation was less than genuine. You've got to sing, so the song goes, like you don't need the money. It's the same with teaching and parenting.

We are not here as adults to make children do things for us. We want them to feel good about *themselves*, so that they will 'buy' into what they feel they need for their own fulfilment. Then when the time comes they will take their own reins and be self-motivated and happy citizens. We want them to have independent souls, to be positive in their outlook, and no matter what they are doing, to be inspired in their lives.

We will not get them to like math unless they are enjoying what they do even if it means that they have outcomes that adults don't expect. We must respect what motivates *them* - it won't be the same things that motivate us.

What the child is doing already is the key. It's the same in business. Databases are gained from activity lists already subscribed to. There is no need for more math, catch-up coaching etc. unless the child requests it. Those days of sweat and tears feeling beneficial, like the castor oil syndrome(if it tastes yuk it must be doing some good), are gone. If the child is interested he will ask for it, and if not he will resist attempts by you to force it onto him.

Teachers, like salespersons, should not feel a need to 'sell' a package. If a child hates fractions, there's nothing wrong with that any more than if he hates pumpkin or if you hate Toyotas. It just means fractions haven't been packaged properly. Marketing has been amiss. You, the adult, assume the perfectly normal right to not buy something because you don't like the box - your child similarly may not like the teacher, the textbook, the classroom environment, the time of the day when the class does fractions or any one of other factors. Yet he may like fractions at other times or places!

> **Hint for the parent of a fraction-hater:**
>
> *Make a pie and cut it into halves, then one half into thirds, then one third into quarters.*
>
> *If they want a piece, they have to ask for it - by the name of the fraction!*

There is a marketing technique known as Prospecting. A vendor will *casually* ask friends if they know of anyone who fulfils the criteria of a customer e.g. if in real estate selling granny flats does anyone know of any grannies looking for a smaller abode? Oh yes, one friend might say, my neighbor has a granny in that situation. Well, may I phone her and quote you as a reference? Yes, sure.

You might call this word-of-mouth but it's more than that. You might call it pushiness or nosiness or you might call up a friend and tell her about a good service you just received. It's all prospecting - linking up, creating pathways of interconnected information and communication which before were in isolated pockets.

Prospecting is very much about math and how it can be spread. Linking is how math works best. Numbers themselves link and unlink. When we learn something new we go from what we know to the next little bit along, the next step. First we identify who or what we know and move outwards. If your child is stuck and can't mentally move, suggest these steps:

- What do you know? Move from there in any direction.
- Is there anything you recognize? Anything at all?.
- Ask someone to give you some start-off information. Ask me or someone else. Who will you ask?

What happens when we walk? We ensure we're standing upright and balanced first. Unless you're on firm ground you can't push forward. Although you're not too sure where the moving foot will land, you do know more about where you were standing prior to take-off. Knowing something about the ground you are on first is everything.

CHILDREN DON'T LEARN BY BEING TAUGHT

Teaching is not about methodology or techniques. It is not about Piaget or Rousseau or any educational philosophy. Neither is it to do with classroom management, assessment systems, curriculum coverage or colorful displays - all gradable reasons to label someone a 'good' teacher.

There are only two reasons why anyone learns or buys anything. This is so for children of any age or adults. It is also so for animals. It is not talked about in teachers' colleges because it is too obvious and too simple, and college professors justifying their employment, droning on about irrelevant education theories and philosophies that come out of books written by bad teachers, don't appear to want to know..

Teaching as we know and call it, means one adult who has decided a body of knowledge is going to be learned come hell or high water, stands and instructs and expects the message to be imparted just because it is that adult's will at that particular time. Adults imagine they have a child before them in what appears to be a receptive capacity. This is could be a gross misread. A child may be sitting still because he is told to, on threat of punishment. This does not make him receptive, and is more likely to make him deceptive. It certainly does not put him in the right mental environment for meaningful and lasting learning to take place. .

Because this is the situation children come to know as the educative process in lieu of anything else calling itself by that name, they are lead to think that if they are going to learn anything it has to be at school, and if they can't learn there then they can't learn anything anywhere else either. If learning doesn't happen they and their significant adults decide they are learning disabled, or have some difficulty. After all, these are 'trained teachers' who should know what they're doing.

Never mind that most young teachers are just children themselves, with no experience of the world, with no carefully honed skills about personal financial management or long and short term interpersonal relationships. The real gut message that everyone on this earth is a teacher for others, which entails showing by example, and being a teacher of and for ourselves necessarily includes at times painful embarrassment leading to self-discovery, is not generously given out by the teaching profession..

What follows now is the secret about why anyone learns anything. It is a two-fold phenomenon and many teachers miss the point of how teaching ever happens.

Teaching occurs when and ONLY WHEN these TWO factors operate. What are they?

1. when a relationship exists between the tutor and the pupil, and
2. when the tutor is interested in the subject.

That's it.

Don't dismiss it on the grounds of simplicity. Think back to all those pop movies like To Sir With Love etc. All the successful teachers are doing these two without too much awareness of why. Yet I sit in school staffrooms and witness the exact opposites on both counts. I hear teachers boasting about how they can't stand this or that pupil, and how they have to take music, or sport after recess, and they hate taking that. If they are telling colleagues that, you can be sure they believe it for themselves and that therefore they are imparting these negatives to their pupils.

If a teacher doesn't like someone, everybody quickly knows - it is in the teacher's body language, tone, mood, and willingness that they don't want to spend time with that person. If the teacher doesn't have any remote interest in a subject it shows - she wants to get it over with as quickly as possible, she's only doing it as part of her job - and the children feel it is a job for them too.

But unless a relationship has been formed between pupil and teacher the pupil won't want to be around that teacher. If he/she doesn't want to be in the teacher's space all efforts by the teacher to impart useful information are mostly doomed. If the child can't physically not be there, he will mentally not be there. On at least one level he will block that teacher. No learning will take place that is of lasting benefit and retention. No joy will accompany that experience, such that the child will make it part of himself.

That is what really happens when you absorb something meaningful. It happens when you go on holiday, by yourself. What happens to you is yours and yours alone to build on and into your experience. No one can take it away and the memories are sweet every time you recall them. That is what true learning is - an absorption which somehow changes you, leaving you richer than you were before.

On the second point, if the teacher is interested in her subject, then that enthusiasm will shine through. Such passion is infectious and before too long everybody in that teacher's life will 'catch' some enthusiasm too. That is what happens in a successful 'performance' or a selling situation.

Think back to a concert you have seen or some recitation, Chances are that you cannot recall the actual songs sung, pieces played, or indeed much content at all. But if you enjoyed the show you will remember the artist's attitude to his art for the love of the instrument shone forth and the energy of the relationship between the artist and his tools was the real joy for the audience. You came away with a love of things you enjoy doing in your *own* life; you came away feeling happy *for* that artist, and you came away with enthusiasm for life on your terms. I'll bet that is what happened, even though at the time it didn't occur to you like that.

That is what the successful teacher does - gives you her enthusiasm, and you convert it to your own. When I was eight my teacher was a Mr. Skellern, and I remember two things about him. The first was when he told us on the last day of the year that his philosophy was to strap someone on the first day of the year so he would have a year of obedience. I remember thinking that was a little unfair on the poor sod who copped it. (Strapping, dear younger readers, was a leather belt wacked across the offender's outstretched hand.)

The second thing I remember about him was his ability to

tell stories. They were real history lessons, but he never called them that. To us they were just yarns about Magellan and his voyaging, and there were pirates and the Spanish Main. Mr Skellern would leap up onto a desk and brandish a would-be sword. He did all the parts, all the voices. It was living theatre. The bell would go but we, the whole class, would plead with him to keep going. No-one wanted to go outside and play.

I look back now and can see what Mr. Skellern did for me. He did not know it, but he gave me a gift, the gift of himself in such a way that I could made it something of my own. He introduced me to enthusiasm and passion for something he loved and loved to share with willing listeners. During that time I scoured the libraries for the C.S. Forrester series about Captain Hornblower. I wanted to continue the adventure started by Skellern in my own mind, and I managed to keep it up successfully too, through endless sea-adventure books, for many happy childhood years afterward.

MAKING IT COUNT

We talk about a quality theatrical performance as 'pure magic'. What we mean is that it took our breath away, it made us gasp, it gave us an emotional reaction. But we should realize that the magic happens INSIDE of us and not on the stage.

When you view any good performance, the dancer, singer, musician, magician, or actor are only moving their bodies in certain ways. There is nothing magical about that unless *we* interpret what we see as magical. We are doing it, not the performer. It is possible to bring these concepts to bear in math.

When you look at any book, what do you see? Not words, not pictures. You merely see dead ink. That's all the eyes rest on. Your *mind* converts them into words, and then into stories, and before long there are images going on in the head; it's all go and you say you 'don't want to put the book down.' But you don't look at a book and think Dead ink, uh more dead ink over here, oh lot's more dead ink on the next page. How boring that would get. The conversion of dead ink into something meaningful is done by you alone.

Similarly when we watch TV we only see moving bits of electricity, but our minds see pictures.

Surely it is the same with a math book. When you see dead ink in the shape of a five, you wouldn't say to yourself 'dead ink in the shape of a five'. Instead you say to yourself FIVE, Hmmm, what does that five mean to me...oh yes, five fingers, five toes, I live at number five, five members of our household etc. You have an understanding of the fiveness of the five, which is understood on an unconscious level.

Perhaps this is painfully obvious. But some children don't get it. Many don't feel the threeness of three, or the hundredness of 100. When you do feel them, you can almost hear them clicking away in your brain when you add them together. When you don't feel them you just stare at the page and sweat. We all should have an instant understanding of numbers when we see them written or hear them spoken. I find children can't read thousands anymore, neither can many teachers. Show them a number like this: 782356 and many adults can't say what it is.

The way to overcome this is for you as a parent to talk openly about the numeracy of things, everyday objects and their groupings, much like The Count in TV's Sesame St, who counts everything he sees.

A child who has command over numeracy will be able to say to himself, "I like myself, I am *one* person amongst many, here is my *place*." You can see it in their play - This goes *here*, and this one goes *there*. The next concept after the sense of one is the sense of *my* one. This is *my* place - I go *here*. This is where the child will learn his *own* identity, his own place in the classroom or family, and following on from that, his rights. Following that will come his respect of the rights of others.

Then comes the child's awareness of how others are treating him. Dignity and justice are all important and he will hit back hard if he feels denied these. Having been given the keys to the city he doesn't want to discover that the locks have been changed.

Counting gives him his identity. Children love to say, "I am five." They don't mean they have been alive for five years, they mean they are 'a five'. Because people say it to them - you are five now, they take it on board as something to *be*. This concept of belonging and the sense of achievement should be reinforced along with the verbal practicing of numeracy recognition. When things he knows and loves have a number concept attached, he will begin to understand numbers, because of their associations. Then he will begin the process of marrying together the world of math and the patterning of his own experiences .

10. PLACE VALUE AND VALUE OF PLACE

In the formative years, hugging a child tells him he is valuable, loving him tells him he is lovable, laughing with him tells him he is special. Smiling at him each day teaches him that the world is a happy place. This is where the math concept of *place value* is born. You can't just say this is what place value means, if the child has not already been given it on a personal level.

Self-esteem comes from self-acceptance. When a parent accords a child the right to be here, and doesn't indicate that most of the time the child is a nuisance, then the child can move himself around in his own mind without tension and he can move ideas and symbolic objects too, rearranging them in new patterns for creative results.

A resentment for math can come from something as tiny as a parent not cuddling a child and saying "I'm glad you're here" often enough.

You as a parent can make changes today, by hugging, saying these words, laughing with the child to make him feel he is fun and funny, thus affirming him back his rights. These will surface in math as confidence, experimentation, less fear of failure, and feeling safe.

Sometimes parents feel they are helping their child by giving him minute by minute feedback on his behavior. "Stop that, DON'T, I said LEAVE THAT ALONE." But what the child takes in is not the verbal content of the message, but the tone and the emotional message, which says "I'm not good enough, I'm not likeable, I'm not considered valuable, my presence here is annoying to someone."

Lacking the language skills to voice his frustration he internalizes it. This is what causes a child to feel rejection and rejection leads to low self-esteem. This leads to diminished confidence for tasks and when it comes to math he won't even try. Because he has learned rejection, his first reaction is to reject any awkward task.

Unnecessary reprimands can cut his math ability clean off at the knees. Instead, you can phrase messages of correction in constructive terms. Whatever we say to children is what they take on as their own internal language when they talk to themselves. Unless they are saying, "I am worthwhile, I am purposeful, I am valuable," they won't be able to say "I'm going to put this here and see what happens..." which is necessary for computational math.

So how do you discipline without criticism? Easy - by separating the child from the task in *your* mind. It is okay to tell him not to do something in a calm quiet way that is reassuring of the love between you. You can continue to smile as you guide his hand away from something hot, you can continue holding him as you take the sharp object away. It is not okay to say he *is* an idiot, a dummy, and someone who always makes mistakes. Because he is not those things - he is a boy, and it is his *behavior* that is faulty, not his existence..

A long time ago a three year old was given a nickname by her father: 'Ten-Naughty-Little-Fingers'. He meant it in fun and in his way of loving. It was funny at the time to all except poor Pam. She changed from an exploring child full of curiosity to being nervy and insecure. I don't think she ever got over the hurt and insensitivity of that name, which persisted for some years. It contributed to some lack of confidence as a young adult. Pam took a while to find her own feet. When she did she shone like a beacon and became a supervisor in a top government job. People loved being in her company. I have always been proud that Pam is my sister.

If you can find a way to ask a child what he wants from a parent, he will probably tell you something like this little list:

1. *"Am I somebody special, am I important to you or not? If I am, why don't you tell me, why won't you spend time with me?"*

You can never tell them too much. Lay it on with a

trowel - you are the best kids ever, we feel we are the luckiest parents in the world to have you because you are such wonderful children. Children will hear this and beam with pleasure. The effect will be greater than you imagine. To adults, words are relatively cheap, but to children, each word counts absolutely and literally.

2. *"Why don't you talk to us in the same nice warm and friendly way you talk to somebody who comes to the door or who rings you up?"*

   Children keenly sense contradictions, and wish the tables were reversed; that you saved your manners for the family and were rude to strangers.

3. *"Am I more important than school? Can I stay home if I don't feel well?"*

   Children often want to test you out to see if you still hold them in the right perspective. They want assurance that you are there for them and not for how well they can perform somewhere. School is not where they belong, and sometimes they sense that parents lose the plot here.

They just want a sign, a tiny indication that they are precious and valuable. of unconditional support come what may. If they say they don't feel well, they are looking for you to put down what you are doing, look at them and express sympathy. Not in an overboard way, but just, "when did it start, where does it hurt, what would you prefer to do today?" They are always looking for that.

If they are valuable then they will feel they are valuable and whatever they do will have some value too. They will take what they do seriously and with some interest in outcomes. They will then take care in their tasks, because the outcomes will also be of value.

From this comes preciseness and accuracy. Otherwise, where will accuracy come from for math tasks? We don't have some accuracy gene. It only comes from learned attitudes to tasks that have value.

Children don't understand when parents say we did this or that for you, so you can have advantages in life. They have nothing to compare their lives with and stories of poverty even appeal to them as preferable lifestyles because all the family was at least together. That's really what children miss and want. They would rather parents did things with them rather than for them. They measure love with attention rather than deeds. This is because children live in a world of emotion, whereas adults are forced by economic requirements to live in a maze of logic.

What's more, children are constantly looking for that closeness, that emotional element in whatever the adult says. Logic or rationality just doesn't feature. Liking them in turn teaches *them* to like things and to be sure in the reliability of life. How can they like anything, especially something like math if they feel that math, just like a person, is not going to like *them* (because they may get answers wrong)?

When the world is essentially a friendly place there is a

far greater chance that everything in it will smile kindly on them.

11. SHOWING THEM UNDERSTANDING

In order to be understood it is necessary for the child to know that the parent is willing to devote time to the task. When the child feels this, an internal message forms that speaks of the parent/child relationship – "she understands me and I understand her." When this is firmly in place, the 'she' can then become the idea of anything. It can be the idea of math. Without this in place there is no confidence of the understanding of a person or a concept.

If you like anything, by definition you have a relationship with it. This is not as clear as it should be in teaching practice. To develop a relationship means you have to attend to a certain body of rules. They apply to parenting, to teaching, to business, and to romantic connection. They even apply to you and your pet. Any relationship must be nurtured, nourished and respected. Changes in the other party must be worked with and compromises agreed to so the union continues. Sensing the importance of the togetherness overrides all other considerations and becomes the guiding light directing everything you do together.

If you as an adult do not have a friendship with the Math World, I suggest that for the sake of your child that you develop one. How? The rules of relationships again. In your mind you can court math as if it was a prospective date. It can be a light-hearted game, but it is serious nonetheless, because if you don't do it your child will not pick up on it and simulate it and so could be disadvantaged.

There are several ways to do this. Decide that the world of numbers is at last going to be available to you in a way that it has not been thus far. Start to notice nice things mathematical, and slowly build on your abilities. Whatever you are interested in *will* have a math area to it;. don't shy from it as you used to, but slowly work through it. Remember all relationships start with a 'date'. Could that be any more mathematical?!

You don't have to fall in love instantly with all of it because real relationships don't work like that either. Rather, a love for math creeps up on you, and the respect strengthens it. Finally it is the understanding and the confidence that gives you the power to operate within a relationship that becomes the sustaining element.

Sometimes the child just wants you to listen. This alone has the power to raise the child's self-esteem, whether that child is 3 or 18. That is also going on in math. For instance, a problem on a page is requiring your attention. It can't speak, but in a sense it does, by the arrangement of words and symbols. It is asking for your participation, should you care to indulge. Taking the time to hear it means, in math terms, exploring what is being required of you. If you feel that all is friendly you will have no problem. But if you feel that it is 'out to get you', there is no way you will cope with it and you will want to run a mile.

Unfortunately the 'out-to-get-you' theme has been the prevailing attitude in the classroom for nearly a century. The long legacy of tests, punishments, overbearingly discipline-conscious administrators and lifeless books and exercises have added up for many children to a bullying academic landscape. Children are expected to cross this mental minefield, stepping carefully but feeling that at any moment they will be gunned down. It doesn't have to be like that.

Here would be my starting list of changes:

- throw away mental arithmetic
- stop times-tables instruction
- ban all compulsory homework of any kind, and replace it with a voluntary system in which the children get paid an hourly rate.
- issue calculators to all children, from four years old onwards
- no more math textbooks in the classroom(put them in the history section in the library)
- start using *real* things instead of symbols, where possible and practicable.
- commandeer the services of children who like math to conduct *I'll-show-you* sessions, in which these children get paid for their services.
- stop all tests, exams, internal assessments, school reports and parent evenings, unless the child requests any of these.

Imagine the excitement from the children if you were to announce that in your school or home, these changes were to be introduced. Schoolwork would at last have a human face and a user-friendliness. Yet much home-schooling is like this.

To expect these changes overnight in schools is a pipe dream and not everyone sees things from this point of view. But even if you reject all of that list, there is much that can and perhaps should be done towards lessening what many children think of as the nightmarishness of math.

AHA, THE SECRET

A common perception is that math as a black art containing deep, dark mysteries that can't be understood by ordinary folk. One way to dispel this belief is to actually present math as magic. Or at least to present some mathematical property disguised as magic. Then follow up by answering their queries of "How's it done?" with the honest reply, "I don't have any special powers; I just know the secret."

Not much separates the person with ability from the one without. No-one is born with any abilities that they cannot acquire if they know where to go. We are all interested in what we can do well. We decide that that is what we like because it comes easiest to us. Because each one of us knows something that others don't in the way of skills, shortcuts and methods; then any subject or study area really can be seen as just a body of secrets.

In math this is especially clear. Given that math is easy so long as you know what to do, if you don't know what to do it could be that you haven't been told the secret yet. Well, this, theoretically at least, is fixable. Just go to the person with the secret and ask them to explain it. This can be a teacher or parent or another child. But as any child will tell you, that's not as easy as it sounds. Teachers and parents think they have done all they can by putting themselves in that available position and they figure that if the child can't come to the party too, that that child has an attitude problem which eventually needs the services of some psychologist or counsellor.

But that's not how children work. They respond to *example*, not to instruction. A child will sit and ponder a problem and let it grind her down before ever thinking of getting up and going over to the teacher to ask her what some secret is.

Children just don't think they have that option, even when they are told they have. They need to see *you* going to get the answer, ringing someone up and asking them, or going to the library and looking it up. From you they get how long one is supposed to ponder a thing before putting into place a strategy to clear the difficulty. The real secret is 3-fold:

a) the knowing that there is a secret that you haven't figured out yet,
b) the knowing you can go ask, and
c) the key to the solution: the explanation itself.

Unfortunately teachers close communication rather than open up new avenues. They don't talk about secrets and they don't recognize what constitute magical keys to understanding and how and when they occur. There are basic rules which work, which are sometimes referred to as lateralism, and which are seldom taught as actual rules.

1) When stuck, move in an entirely new way.
2) Leave something you can't figure out and come back to it later.
3) Try many things, just for the sheer hell of it, to see what will happen.
4) If stuck, look for an opposite solution to what is expected - this often works.
5) Go through all the possible answers.
6) Give up and move on. (Perfectly valid - ask the 50,000 divorcees every year)

When I was a classroom teacher, I found the students I tried my approaches on were willing to try to find these elements on their own, to discover whatever was the Secret. In this way, my performance grabbed them, and what was hidden in the magic was what I wanted them thinking about.

It was important that they realized that no-one has special powers; not magicians, psychics, mathematicians, nor clairvoyants. All these people use secrets. Most magicians can duplicate any psychic phenomenon. To quote James Randi when exposing Uri Geller, "if anyone says he is using divine powers, he is doing it the hard way."

The value of the notion of secrets is that children warm to them. Secret clubs (remember the Secret Seven?), secret messages passed around the class about who's in love with whom, secret rendezvous with your beloved; all this captures the childhood imagination. Perhaps the thrills of shining the torch under the bedclothes and building inaccessible forts and huts underground and in trees are throwbacks to a womb-darkness-security.

Whatever the origins, secrets *work*. Try it on a child. Present a problem and then ask if the child would like the *explanation* or the *secret*. Both are exactly the same, but the child will choose 'the secret' every time. It's far more romantic and is a word in the child's world rather than that of the adult.

I believe this approach keeps the interest and attention of the class in a way the old system doesn't. It costs nothing other than the changes of some words, and if you have the choice it is better to utilize ideas that a child will better respond to.

Secrets are fundamental to life and to love in a literal sense too. The word 'secret' comes from *se*, meaning self, something apart, something special and precious. That is the status within us that understanding achieves, and is still the perception of what a good education is in the minds of poor people. I believe the concept is a healthy one and is to be encouraged. It embodies curiosity, excitement and discovery.

I know someone who took Spanish I at university, just for the excitement of it, when she was in her sixties. She got an A+. Did she go on to the next level? No - she liked the course, the books and tutors so much she took the same course again the following year!

Passion always takes precedence over practicality. Secrets evoke passion, explanations do not. Anything that accesses the imagination has some link to secrecy. Stories beg to be told, and once out in the open they lose most of their value. Information is like that too. An idea everyone is aware of ceases to be of interest, as is an old previously learned fact. It is the new and the novel that excites, and a mystery revealed is the breaking of an instant news story, if only in one person's head.

Math can be presented as a whole body of secrets. Children will not tire of it if this approach remains consistent. It was only a couple of thousand years ago that a ruling intellectual elite, the so-called Pythagorean School of Mathematics, actually passed laws prohibiting news of paradoxes and unsolved math riddles from reaching the ears of the common folk, lest they revolt against the body of eminent scholars in whom they had placed great faith.

The idea of secrets constituting knowledge persists somewhat today in the type of language employed by doctors, lawyers, politicians and auto-mechanics, who do not want lay folk to understand too much or they might stop paying out and start doing things themselves. Certainly this originated with the early monks, who jealously guarded their monopoly of access to the body of knowledge contained in sacred books. There is nothing so powerful as one person holding out on a secret and another person wishing to be told it.

BOYS' MATH AND GIRLS' MATH

Studies have been undertaken by teachers and sociologists that reflect on general gender differences. One has involved 991 Dunedin 5 year olds. Boys are better at doing one thing at a time; girls are better at doing many things at once. While girls are fond of detail, boys like things to be simply put - they may give up earlier when there are too many instructions.

It was noted that young boys are more upset at being separated from their mother. They are shyer, less confident, more dependent. They have a shorter attention span, give up on things more easily, and have less frustration tolerance. It has also been observed that they are also more hyperactive, more restless, fidget more than girls, destroy property more often, and have more tics. They are more difficult to manage and more inclined to bully others. Girls, on the other hand, when separated from their mother are more often miserable, bite their nails more often, and develop fussier natures.

Girls do more puzzles, boys play more in sandpits. When taken into a garden, boys more typically will want to dig holes in it and girls will prefer to pick the flowers.

Apart from the finding that there is no difference between the sexes in child studies when it comes to telling lies, girls are generally ahead of boys in all aspects of language development for at least the first five years of school life. Much confidence in early math years comes from ease in the use of the appropriate language. Boys may often understand the processes more, but they may fall short of being able to adequately describe them. Because the language gets selectively reinforced, boys can lose heart and can end up thinking they're no good at math.

Workability is more the girls' aim; knowing how to get a result that will please the teacher, after which they can move on to the next thing that comes up. It's not quite the same as understanding a process. Girls are culturally encouraged to be group-aware and relationship-oriented. This bodes well in learning sets and points out some reasons for perceived gender differences in math skills. In social as well as math situations, girls often only want to know what they have to say and to whom, to get themselves included, to be part of the group. They want to know the lay of the land, the state of the problem and how they fit in, in terms of being able to find solutions.

Boys are less concerned with pleasing; they seek to know what happens. Rather than examining while leaving things be, they want to make changes, apply movement, shift gear, look at inner workings, and take things apart. The interest is in how they work and not *that* they work. They want to do it without necessarily talking about doing it.

In co-ed high schools teachers have noted the difference when it comes to computers. Boys rush to the machines whilst girls are not in such a hurry - they can't talk to each other operating keyboards; it is not a social activity. Boys on the other hand, prefer to work by themselves in relative silence.

I used to notice that girls, when allowed to sit and work together, say to each other, "Oh, I can't do this, can you?" all the while doing it. The opportunities to converse seems more attractive to females. This is not to say that boys don't like talking. But their preference seems to be more in the doing.

Few young girls try to wreck their dolls and many women can show you dolls they had as young children, whereas boys can point to few intact toys surviving from early childhood. When you take something apart you often lose the point of it, because if the exercise fails and you end up not understanding a function, you've lost the original article as well. When a boy wrecks a new toy, it is not that he is a vandal, merely curious and exploratory. It is more the fault of the toy than of him if it breaks too soon after purchase. Better to provide such a child with equipment designed to be taken apart..

It also might explain why children leave messes on their floor. The joy is in the disassembly - there is far less to be learned from putting it all back again. Going somewhere is always more fun than returning home.

Because they often think some knowledge of the inner working mechanism is required of them, boys are more liable to make more of a math problem than might really exist. While the boy may still be pondering the deep implications of some question, the girl in the next seat may have worked the same problem to what she thinks will be an acceptable answer and handed it in, hoping for praise. From her maternal role model, the girl may approach math like housework; she rolls up her sleeves and wades in. There might not be much wonder involved. Yet for a boy, unless some hunting element, some sense of elusiveness is there, a task often doesn't seem worth pursuing.

In the early years, girls are across the board better at math than boys, according to the way we assess academic progress. Boys are separated from the father, the preferred role-model, at an early age. It has been suggested that at an inexpressible level they resent that the mother is there instead. For girls there is no problem - the preferred role-model is available. Thus boys hesitate and their identity development misses a beat or two, whilst girls, having no identity factor to work at, pass them academically. Boys see school as a place full of women, and so won't apply themselves as well as girls.

It is unfortunate that boys are not rewarded for daydreaming and dawdling. It is also unfortunate that as girls grow older, society gradually steers them away from math-based careers. Yet research has shown that when girls are expected to do well in math and to continue to choose math-oriented options, they continue to beat the boys at ALL levels.

If a boy is falling behind everyone says to him, "What? You have to work harder - math is VERY important," whereas if a girl falls behind the common reaction from the adults in her life is, "Oh well, she's not going to be a famous scientist, is she! She'll probably leave school and just get married."

Math gets lumped in with science, and language with the arts: a polarity that has always suited school administrations more than what actually happens in life. There is no reason why art and math should not enjoy a double-billing – for example the study of linguistics is highly scientific. But when children approach option crossroads and are forced to decide, it is the boys who are encouraged to take the hi-fi road and the girls who take what is left. Science is the area that gets the research funds, so in the long run the boys benefit and land the more lucrative jobs.

The end result is a society that invents industry-sponsored big toys like NASA projects that sometimes exist for their own engineering feats. The technology ends up serving itself rather than the common people, and the machines can end up working for the fantasies of collective male corporate management rather than for the nation's best welfare.

The task for boys who might be having trouble coping with math is to see that much math is just verbal in its requirement. When you see a boy taking something apart, it is worth seizing the opportunity to create a math exercise. Ask him casually how many bits he's ended up with and therefore how many parts to the whole. Engage him in conversation about it on any level. Slowly get him used to the language of math - what goes before this, after that, what was the first part removed and what will be the last, what needs to be taken away or added. How many times can he assemble or dismember in a certain time frame, say, 5 minutes?

These are essential number line concepts. Get him used to the fact that no more is required of him at this stage than description and possibility, and lighten his mental load. Offer small rewards. So long as language is being used and he's enjoying it he will want to do it again, which means you can hook in some more direct language in the next session.

One possible solution for girls experiencing difficulties

may be to see that understanding is required and talking should, in math at least, be to unravel understanding and not be a substitute for working at a solution.

If a child is talking too much and not thinking enough and used to calling out immediately to you for help - you might now decide to be busy and unavailable for longer and longer periods or stay just out of earshot.

Also as a teacher or parent there is no need to always react to everything she says. Rather than existing for relaying important information, chatter is often just used as a binding social glue.

MATH AND MAGIC

The purpose of magic has always been to leave audiences wondering what happened. A good magician doesn't usually leave *enough* clues for the spectator to exactly determine what happened. That doesn't mean that a successful magical presentation will prevent the viewers from constructing some explanation. In fact it should cause the audience to find many possible explanations.

The explanations don't necessarily lead to practical solutions. As a practicing magician I am aware of the ethics surrounding exposure. There are TV programs that claim to reveal magical secrets, and there are magicians who complain that these programs do the art of magic a disservice. My view is quite the opposite - I think it helps the art. No magician in his right mind would do a trick that had just been exposed on TV the night before, using that particular method. His audience would be unaware that there was more than one method and would come along because they felt sure they had sussed him out.

We have already discussed secrets in math. If the exposing of some secrets in magic helps children become motivated to uncover secrets in their own way, away from the formal magic arena, then the exercise of exposing for a magician who finds himself in a teaching environment is worthwhile. I doubt if any magician's livelihood could be threatened by any small measure of exposure a teacher would be providing to his class.

There is always more than one method, more than one answer, and more than one solution to a problem. Math and magic meet where both access the imagination and both challenge the viewer's knowledge of the world and its workings.

Anyone daring enough to stand in front of a class can be a performer. Anyone willing to suspend reality momentarily can present magic. It is not the tricks that are important, rather the sense of discovery that comes from the exercise and the rapport and communication skills capable of being explored by the class and teacher.

That is precisely what happened in the teaching cases I've mentioned in the next pages. The class in question took off with the material presented and found their own explanations, thought through and discussed what they saw, and in some cases came up with their own modifications to the effects presented, all while practicing basic arithmetic skills and problem-solving strategies. Best of all, they did it without being asked. They did it because they were interested.

As a math teacher you want the class to find explanations for everything you show them. Children get so involved with the 'magic' that they go and perform it for others, keeping the secrets to themselves. Following are two presentations for a couple of old mathematical tricks that have been performed by many magicians. They both fall into the category of mental magic. This is a realm where the magic appears to happen without the use of props, entirely under the control of the mentalist's mind powers. In reality, simple math is involved. (acknowledgement to Larry Moss)

One student follows the steps at the blackboard, while I face the back of the room, unable to see what is being written. The class work well together to check each other's answers. As an extra precaution, the co-operating teacher in the room keeps an eye on the process to ensure that everything is done correctly.

1. DICTIONARY PREDICTION

"As everyone walked into class today I was trying to sense patterns in brainwaves. I feel so confident in my ability to sense the way all of you think, that I wrote down a prediction and sealed it inside this envelope."

I hand out the envelope for one person to hold, but not open. "I would like one person to stand at the blackboard and follow some basic directions."

I pick from a vast selection of anxious volunteers.

"Write any 3 digit number on the board. Directly underneath it, write the number with the digits reversed. If you started with 123, the new number you wrote is 321. Now find the difference between the number you started with and the new number. Once again, I'd like you to reverse the digits of this latest number. Add these last two numbers together.

"What's left on the board is probably a big number. This number indicates a page and the place on a book in this classroom."

I then pick someone in the class to pick up the dictionary on a nearby table. "How many digits are in the number on the board?"

When they answer, "four," I tell them to use the first three digits as the page number and to use the last digit as the number of words to count down on the page. I turn now for the first time to the board and instruct, "turn to page 108, and read the ninth word on the page." When the word is read, I ask the person holding the prediction to open the envelope and read the contents to the class.

Inside is written that very word.

DISCUSSION

This effect is based on the 9's complement property of base 10 arithmetic. We can start with any three digit number, provided that the number is different when it is reversed. When we find the difference between the two numbers we will always end up with a number for which the outer digits add to 9 and the middle digit is 9. Therefore, the second step will always yield 1089. For instance:

851 -158 = 693

693+396 = 1089

The principle here can be explored closely with the students. When they perform the sequence on their own several times with different numbers they will discover patterns. It can also be explored with 2 and 4 digit numbers to see what results the students find.

Turning this into a prediction makes it all seem magical since I somehow knew what word we would find in the dictionary. Having the end result be a word in some book in the back of the room adds another level of mystery until this problem is explored. Once everyone realizes that we always end up with the same number, they can conclude that I looked in the dictionary ahead of time.

Because the aim of math should be about understanding, it is probably of the greatest value for a teacher doing this to work out with the class the explanation of this principle. However a brief explanation is here provided.

EXPLANATION

No matter what 3-digit number you or anyone else chooses in this game, the final result will always be 1089. Why? Let abc denote the unknown 3-digit number. Algebraically, this is equal to:

$$100a + 10b + c$$

When you reverse the number and subtract it from the original number you get the number cba, algebraically equal to:

$$100c + 10b + a$$

Upon subtracting abc - cba, you get:

$$100a + 10b + c -(100c + 10b + a) = 100(a-c) + (c-a) = 99 (a-c)$$

Hence after subtracting in step 2, we must have one of the following multiples of 99; that is: 099, 198, 297, 396, 495, 594, 693, 792, or 891, all of which produce 1089 after adding it to the reverse of itself in step 3.

Why outer digits add to 9

To find why adding the outer digits in step 2 always results in 9, let's look first at a simplified, but generic case with only a two digit number, ab, where a and b each represent a single digit.

We write the number, reverse it, and find the difference:

$$ab - ba = cd$$

We would write the equation such that $ab > ba$. Then we know that $d = 10 + (b - a) = 10 - (a - b)$, and $c = (a-1) - b = 1 + (a-b)$.

If this isn't obvious, remember that to subtract a from b we need to borrow from the ten's place. We end up subtracting a from $10 + b$. That also explains the 1 in the calculation of c.

I suggested above that adding the outer digits of the solution, in this case c and d, would produce 9, as we can see here:

$$10-(a-b) - 1+(a-b) = 9$$

The idea is the same for a three digit number. The only limitation on this is that we use a number that is different when it is reversed.

VARIATION 1

An allied trick is to take any number of any number of digits, say 45382, and rewrite the number underneath in any jumbled order, just so long as the larger number is on top. Then subtract them, e.g.:

45382 -24853 = 20529

The answer will have digits that add to make 9, even if you have to add them a couple of times. This is called resolving them to one digit. In this case, 2+0+5+2+9 = 18, and 1+8 = 9.

In presenting this effect, your head is turned away from the blackboard the whole time. When your subject has a result, get him to rub out everything except the answer. Then instruct him to circle one of the digits in the answer, and read aloud to you the other digits. So if he circles the 5,

2 0 5 2 9

he would read two, zero, two... and nine. You announce immediately that he has circled a five! How you the HECK did you know that? Well, all the digits in the answer will add to 9. As he reads the other digits, you add them in your head. When he has said them all you subtract the total from 9, or the nearest multiple of 9. The answer will be the circled digit.

VARIATION 2

Write any number (of any number of digits) down twice with one above the other, add a zero to the top one, and subtract the lower from it. e.g.:

67850 -6785 = 61065

Once again the result will have digits that add to 9.

2. ANIMALS IN THE WORLD

VARIATION 1

"I am going to plant a thought in your minds. This is a large class, so I'm not sure I can get it exactly right. One or two of you may get a slightly different picture than the others. Work with me and concentrate so my thoughts can be planted in your mind.

"Pick a number. Any number will do, but a small one may be easiest. Write that number on the blackboard. That's not actually the number we're going to use though. We're going to use that to find another number that's different from what all of us were thinking of to begin with.

"Double the number you've selected. Add the number 8. Divide the new number by two. Subtract the number you started with from the number you have now. Find the letter in the alphabet that corresponds to that number. That is, if you have a 1, the letter you should be thinking of is `A'. If the number you have now is 2, use the letter `B', 3 is `C', 4 is `D', 5 is `E'. Continue through the alphabet until you reach your number.

"Think of a country whose name starts with the letter you are at. Take the second letter in the country name, and find an animal that lives in that country. Think of the color of that animal.

"Now, if everyone has been concentrating, you should all be thinking of the same animal as me. But actually, I think something went wrong. I'm sensing that you're all thinking of the same animal, but what I'm sensing doesn't make much sense. There are no grey elephants in Denmark."

VARIATION 2

We may want to reach the same result by a slightly different method.

Pick a number. Multiply by 9. Add the digits together. If the result of adding the digits contains more than one digit, add the digits again. Continue doing this until you have a single digit number. In other words, if the answer you ended up with was 98 when you multiplied, you would add 9 and 8 to get 17. You would then add 1 and 7 to get 8. Now subtract 5 from the number remaining.'

As for variation 1 they would be instructed to find the letter in the alphabet corresponding to their number and continue as earlier to end up with grey elephants in Denmark.

DISCUSSION

The steps of method 1 can be written out algebraically. Let's use n for the number selected. Then, written more concisely, the result is obtained with

$$\frac{2n+8}{2} - n.$$

That simplifies to $n + 4 - n$.

The result is clearly 4.

When done quickly there isn't much time to think about a

country. In fact, if you give it some thought you'll realize that there aren't very many choices. Denmark is chosen most often. The same goes for animals starting with "E." That doesn't mean others won't arise. Sometimes they do and sometimes mistakes are made.

But you can usually cover for the error by indicating just how close you came. In fact, often the audience is more impressed when you miss. Near misses indicate that your method isn't fool proof, but that you do know what you're doing.

The second method presented is based on 9's complement. it's a simple rule of the base 10 number system that when you multiply a number by 9, the result of the added digits is also 9. You can now subtract any number you like in order to have the audience using any letter from "A" through "I".

When this was presented in class, both methods were used, one after the other. You want the students to conclude that you used a mathematical trick, but by changing methods, you make the path to finding an explanation a bit more challenging. They don't realize at first that you use different methods. Once the basics are understood, you can end with any number you like.

Most students now are familiar with non-traditional, student-centered, inquiry-based instruction in math due to the new math curriculum. If not and you are keen enough and can get a kind soul to do your playground duties, you might like to establish a "math lab" in the school.

The math lab can be available to all students on a voluntary basis during their lunch period. In addition to this, the teacher of the class discussed here might like to teach a Fun Friday lesson at the end of each week. This lesson is intended to be more enjoyable and less structured than their typical lessons. The lessons discussed here can used to bring inquiry into the classroom during these Fun Friday periods. The students that attend the lunchtime sessions can go back to their classes and perform what they discover. This can encourage the whole class to participate at some level or other.

CARD TRICKS

One aspect I believe to be valid to math is the world of card tricks. Almost all children love to perform these in front of the class. Even children who have poor social skills and who wouldn't be seen dead reading a passage of an English story, will get out in front of everybody and show a trick his uncle taught him. These tricks can be analyzed, with the permission of the performer, and explanations shared.

CONCEPTS EXPLORED, CLASS REACTIONS

Having an arsenal of magic to throw at a class is wonderful, but what does it accomplish? Most notably, it has students concentrating on mathematical skills in a way that interests them. In these examples, they weren't doing arithmetic just because they had a list of problems to get done for a grading, they were doing it because it was posed as an interesting problem; a problem that they formulated themselves from the presentation they saw and therefore worth doing because some intrigue presented itself.. When children can see some point to working something out, they will pursue it with vigor. The student will be able to go home and try them on members of the family.

During the process, they worked with other students around them to discuss solutions, practiced basic arithmetic skills, learned more about the base ten number system, and drew their own conclusions about the relationships between numbers.

Even more importantly, they established their own goal. They saw something that was "magic" and they wanted to know how it worked. That question was on their minds before they ever started discussing a solution.

FURTHER NOTES ON THE CLASSROOM EXPERIENCE:

I started with the dictionary prediction. Not surprisingly, the students didn't know how to approach their initial question of how the effect works. As far as I am aware they had no previous experience debunking psychic demonstrations. Rather than providing scaffolding right from the beginning, I suggested we try to repeat this.

We picked another number, followed the same steps, and came up with the same answer. The class was surprised by this, and several suggested we try different numbers until we get a different answer. We tried again. After a few attempts, one student proudly declared that the trick works because we always get the same answer when we follow those steps. Heads shook in agreement. Many seemed satisfied, but some called out questions along the lines of, "but why do we always get the same answer?" I was quite happy to see that after they answered their question, they chose on their own to probe deeper.

Looking around the room, I could see that many of the students were still scratching at their papers trying new numbers. After a few minutes went by, one student announced that it didn't always work. He found a number that just gave him 0. He told me his number and I worked it out with the class at the blackboard.

I did not immediately write in my notes what the number was, but at the completion of the lesson I did recall that it was a palindrome with a middle digit of 0. The students wanted to know if the 0 in the middle was the reason the trick failed. In answer to that question, we tried a number of my choosing with 0 in the middle. It worked for me.

I soon realized that my choosing a number wasn't a good idea. Students suggested that since it was my trick I picked a number that I knew would work. I did know it would work, but not because I memorized a set of numbers that we could use. Up until this point, things were going well without my active participation. There seemed little reason to jump in now, as long as they were still progressing. With that realization, I stepped back and continued to write only what they asked me to write.

It wasn't long before they decided that the numbers that weren't working were ones with the same first and last digit. Interestingly, it took a bit longer to conclude that the problem was connected with the number being the same when it was reversed. I had to ask prompting questions like, "Why does it matter if the first and last digit are the same?"

We discussed this for a while, and I asked more questions than I answered. It was necessary for me to suggest that they look at the numbers at each step, rather than do the whole series of steps each time. I started the sequence again with one of the numbers we had before, and stopped after doing the subtraction. I immediately started on another three digit number without completing the first. "Does anyone see a pattern?"

This question started them comparing the numbers. Almost immediately, one student pointed out that in every problem we did, the middle digit was nine. Others apparently looked for more nines and found that the outer digits added to nine.

At each step of the way, as we progressed, the students found it necessary to test their theories. They checked numbers by hand and with calculators. Despite the fact that we had success in explaining things so far, the students preferred to prove this rule empirically. It was actually difficult to stop them from trying it endlessly.

At last I asked a question that I thought would put an end to their search for a number that would break the rule: "How many numbers would we have to test if we wanted to try all of the three digit numbers that are different when we reverse them?"

Various answers came from them. "1000." "900." "999." "10." Each answer called out could be explained by the students that suggested them. We were out of time and I suggested that question if they wanted some homework. I do not push homework and didn't expect a complete or accurate answer from any of them. I did expect some creative thinking.

I received many interesting answers, along with pages full of numbers that they tried. They wanted to prove to me that this really works on everything that they could try. Some even apologized for running out of time and not testing more numbers. Checking numbers like that isn't what I intended for them, but seeing the group this enthusiastic over math was exciting.

The best part of this is that I know they took what they learned out of class with them. Most of them tried it on friends and family members and reported back how successful they were. The only significant difficulty is that I concentrated on the mathematical aspect of this and forgot to tell the students that not all dictionaries would have the same words on page 108!

Far more could be explored just from this problem. I decided however, to abandon this particular item, and pick up a different trick the following week. Had I pursued this, I would have spent more time discussing the property of nines that allows this to work. I would have worked with the students to develop ways of using this property as a shortcut for doing arithmetic.

We spoke some about the difficulty of testing every number and the reason why it's better to prove this is true without trying it. However, to satisfy their curiosity, it would not have been difficult to test all numbers on a computer. As a further exercise, I would have liked to try this with two and four digit numbers to see if the students could develop more general explanations for what they saw.

The second effect was received as well as the first. In fact, for a week I had been answering the question, "When will we do more magic?" I presented the effect using both methods described here, we discussed it, and then we repeated it. Having already been through this experience they already knew what was expected and they started offering explanations. The simple algebraic representation that this problem has is of no value to students that haven't yet been exposed to algebra. This proved to be a more difficult problem for the students to crack than the first.

As before, they approached it from an empirical standpoint. In this case however, I pointed out that I would let them use any number they wanted. Therefore, no matter how long they tried testing numbers, they couldn't test everything. Many still expressed a belief that eventually they would find a number that didn't work.

I provided one hint for them. I suggested that I could make them come up with any letter of the alphabet. That was the key to cracking this puzzle. "What happens if you use a different number?" asked one student. We proceeded to try different numbers in place of the 8 in the initial instructions.

Over time, other things came out, like we were multiplying by two and dividing by two. Eventually it was concluded that the number we would end with would be half of the number we add.

The entire process, as with the dictionary prediction, fit within one 45 minute period. We did not have an opportunity to try adding odd numbers, or multiplying and dividing by numbers other than two. Instead, I let this lesson also rest at the end of the period, allowing them to explore further on their own and to try it on friends and parents.

As I expected from the previous experience, the students enjoyed the exercise enough that they were happy to report back how their attempts at being magicians worked out.

SUMMARY

The most important thing to be learned from this is that students will pick up and explore material that interests them. Although I went into these lessons with ideas of things I wanted to explore and in some cases I got to cover the material that interested me; in other cases, I had to completely change my way of thinking to match the students and to look at what they wanted to look at. Any time I chose to ask my own questions, rather than follow theirs, I felt that I was in danger of losing their attention.

I am convinced that magic is a wonderful way of making math come alive for students. It allows for a true inquiry environment for learning. The questions are built into the material, and students are happy to explore them on their own. Rather than being a sleight of hand, math takes on the appearance of something far grander - something that is always there and waiting to be discovered - in a sense a sleight of nature.

THE MONEY GAME

This started, as far as we know, in the year New Zealand decided to change its currency notes. Country-wide competitions had been held amongst professional graphic designers and the winning note designs had been selected. The nation was buzzing with expectation over the soon-to-be released new currency.

As a class art exercise, teacher Terry Sheffield, in a little country school in Owhata, near Taupo, instigated a class competition for new note designs. Entries were submitted and the winners were chosen fairly by a judging board elected from within the class.

As a final reward for a project well accomplished, Terry. photocopied off enough of the winning designed notes for everyone in the class to have $100 worth. Class members put the bunch of notes in their desks and left them there. Some colored them in. Everyone assumed that was that.

About a week after this exercise was all but forgotten, one pupil wandered across the classroom to see his mate.

"Hey, lend us your ruler?"

"It'll cost you."

"How much?"

"5 dollars class money"

The first boy went to his desk, undid the rubber band and pulled out a class five. "I want a receipt!"

The second boy wrote him one out, but the first felt the only way to restore the balance was to charge someone else something. The ball began rolling. Terry Sheffield was quick to pick up on what was happening. Partly because kids were starting to go bananas charging each other for nonsense things, like moving along a long seat to let the other in. There was no way to recall the money. The next day he launched a discussion.

"Regarding the money we made," he began. "We've all got some left in our desks. Let's do something with it. I have decided on some charges we might impose on ourselves, and some rules and some pay-outs for rewards. Let me read you what I have been thinking of and see if you all approve. We can discuss it and then put the ideas to the vote."

That's how it began. I met Terry when I found myself up in the Far North performing my math/magic shows at the Okaihau District School. Terry had just been appointed the new principal. When I learned his name, I instantly recognized it from his brief article that I had come across some time before about the Money Game, as Terry had called it in the article. I was thrilled to meet him and ask him about it first-hand.

Apparently it was a thing that fired up the imagination of every child in the class. Helen Varney (who also read the same article) found the same enthusiasm when she ran her version of the money game in her Vauxhall School class in Devonport. The kids couldn't wait to get to school. Attendance was never better. It was all anyone seemed to talk about.

Terry was initially taken aback at the enthusiasm with which most children got into it. It didn't matter that they could only use the money in the classroom. It was their money. in their minds, as if they were dealing with precious life savings .

Terry's class decided that each person would receive a further $15 per week. Some lucky students who had photocopiers at home saw counterfeiting as a possibility, but Terry was insistent that all notes had to carry his personal signature written with his pen. All transactions had to be written up as profit/loss statements. Weekly balances had to be maintained and balances carried forward. If basic bookkeeping was not done, new money for the next week was not issued.

Goods and services were bought or rented from each other. Services performed were either at a fixed rate or negotiable. Interestingly, politicians please note, GST was considered and put to the vote but thrown out in favour of an equal tax system, imposed weekly.

Taxes paid for essential services, like the Class Court and went towards expenses of a break-up party on the last day of term. The Judge received a small financial incentive, as did monitors, and these were elected positions and renewed monthly. Fines were imposed; for instance, running in the classroom was considered 'speeding', whilst sitting on someone else's seat without permission was 'unlawful parking.'

Terry charged a basic desk rent of $5 per week. A "desk with a view" (by the window, or up at the front) cost an extra dollar. The children were paid for attending school. Basic stationery was supplied, paid for by taxes. Special projects could apply for a Research Grant for more materials.

As wealth accumulated, the class perceived the need for a Bank, and an Insurance scheme, lest money be lost or stolen. This proved good fodder for class discussion. Who was to be banker? Many volunteered. The best way, said Terry, was for those interested to submit a resume. A valuable lesson followed as to what constituted a good resume.

One boy really wanted to be banker. His father and mother were both accountants. So he went to some trouble to win selection. He went to the local ASB and persuaded the manager to write him a reference. It read, "this boy is a regular saver and is known to our staff as a friendly, courteous and conscientious young man. We have no hesitation in recommending him to any financial office in your classroom."

As no-one else had gone to this much trouble, it was decided that he was probably the most motivated, and therefore would be good at the job. He got it.

It was noticed that at week's end the same people appeared to have more money than the rest. Equally, there was a group who were always broke. Out of class discussion it was decided that a Citizens' Advice Bureau was needed. This took the form of a panel discussion, and the panel members were selected from the top ten 'earners'. A Social Welfare system was rejected; nobody wanted undue attention directed toward the poorer members.

Some borrowed from the Bank, which of course charged an interest rate. Conversely, deposits earned interest. Interest was calculated and processed weekly. The Bank also decided to issue mortgages to those who qualified, who showed deposit histories and income steadiness.

What could be bought? School buildings were for sale, shops just down the road, and houses on the other side of the street. These were hypothetical sales, but deeds were printed up and properties were advertised when the teacher decided they had come onto the market. Property prices were very fair - nothing exceeded $200. Deeds were considered money in the bank and could be sold anytime for their purchase price. The bank issued an appreciation of percentage of the original purchase price for the first week which compounded in succeeding weeks.

The local bank manager kept close to what was happening and was personally intrigued. He offered to come and talk to the class about bank interest rates in the real world. This proved very popular. The class knew what he was talking about! Then one class member invited her father along, who was in real estate! His talk was even better, and he recounted some of his experiences and gave advice on investment. Once again, everybody knew what he was talking about.

The excitement spread to the class next door, who decided to do their own money too. But they opted for $150 each to start off and $20 each per week. Clearly now an exchange rate was necessary and was accordingly implemented for transactions between classes.

An auction was organized by the first class. Everybody brought junk and no-longer-used toys to contribute. The other class was invited and this put more money into circulation.

The Money Game ran for two terms. School holidays

finally killed its momentum. All along it was stressed that it was only a game.

The main advantage to come from it was the feeling of power the children felt over their own lives and confidence that came from owning their own. New pecking orders were established and some children discovered inherent skills within themselves that they were previously unaware of. What was interesting too was that children who had not shone at all before the unit started, and who became somewhat high profile during it, remained up in their own esteem and in the opinions of others when the study unit ceased to operate.

Most staff and parents were surprised that the game generated such enthusiasm. Homes became places of hot discussion as excited children planned money-making schemes. Some homes also established money games of their own and had systems of turning house money into real cash. Parents found themselves asking, "If you clean my windows, what would you charge?" Negotiating would get the price down. (If the game ended then and there at least a couple of mums got some windows done for the cost of some Xeroxing!)

Although it worked in class where children paid desk rent, of course one cannot charge children at home room and board at the age of 8. However, the money game has worked in some homes where family discussion has decided what things should be provided free and what comes under the house money system.

EXERCISES:

- Make charts of weekly transactions.
- Create receipts and invoice order forms.
- See what the end of the week totals are.
- Bring balances brought forward to the next week's trading.
- Keep transaction sheets.
- Someone in the family should act as banker.
- Rotate the duty. What qualities does a banker need?
- Discuss a time when banking occurs.
- Pay the banker a wage for services. Bank has to have a name, say the Williams Family Bank.
- In order to interchange money between family banks an exchange rate has to be worked out.
- Banks can issue loans. And there are interest rates.

Terry's advice was don't rush into the Money Game. Aspects of it will develop as ideas occur. Let the children themselves come up with the extensions. But make a start somewhere.. Once you start talking about interest rates etc. they'll start noticing things when they go into real banks.

All services offered can come into the money game, like room cleaning or picking toys up from the floor. If you charge for meals they can negotiate second helpings. Package deals and specials can be offered in bargain weeks. This helps to establish consistency of price levels, and price controls can give the child spending and practice at financial planning confidence. Inflation can match that in the outside world.

The bank can offer savings incentives on fixed deposits. Insurance companies can be run.

If you run it at all, everyone in the family should participate in the money game. Real money too can flow into the family. If outside money flows in because of services the family performs, some of it can be earmarked for the family bank and translated into dividends for everyone in terms of real wealth. An internal exchange rate of family money/real money would then be involved.

Make all transactions, services, charges etc. simple and rounded off amounts for easy computations.

HOW TO RETAIN CONTROL

Perhaps you are now throwing up your hands in horror and thinking this all seems such a headache. But it isn't. The point is that it remains child inspired and largely child-run. And by virtue of the fact that your imagination has instigated the game and the discussions means you are in control. It is always important that the child learns some measure of control over his/her life. The Money Game can provide that. Control comes from self-control; which comes from the parental role model. Discipline is *not* control - it causes fear.

HOW SCHOOLS CAN EARN REAL MONEY

Today, up and down the country, schools battle scarcity of funding and the rising costs of services that must come from yearly bulk allowances. Added to that are low teacher wages and governmental disinterest in making schools fully resourced. Schools could be vital living centers of the community, a role that in years past they enjoyed. But these days they must look to innovative ways to raise funds themselves. Gala Days were one accepted way in the past.

Today these face competition from weekend markets, garage sales and other schools' events. Some schemes are worth looking at as ways of raising funds.

Panama School, in South Auckland, is located in the vicinity of shops and businesses. They have sold street forefront space for advertising hoardings. Other schools have (despite community opposition) sold Telecom the permission to erect transmitting aerials.

Some schools print a yearly calendar with business ads around the calendar section.

MAKING USE OF THE FOYER

There is no reason why foyers, which are public spaces, should not be turned into shops; after all, schools are trading places already - books are purchased, and raffle tickets, money is brought by children to see travelling performers etc. The office is often a place where money is counted.

Oram School, in the Bay of Plenty, is running a household products stall in the foyer. A parent with business experience is running it and extracting wages from the profits, with an equal percentage going to the school.

A foyer bookshop could be run in the same way.

At Colwill School can be seen The School Souvenir Shop. Gifts to send relatives overseas or to give locally for birthdays etc. can come from here. Children can make extraordinarily beautiful paintings, Xmas Cards, etc. Whilst one would not like to see schools become child labor camps, artwork that is normally thrown out instead makes its way to the School Souvenir Shop. A teacher aide is usefully employed putting paintings that are saleable into cardboard frames, and displaying and pricing clay models.

Trade Aid shops have this feeling when you go inside them. The prices are cheap and one feels good that spending a gift dollar in such a shop is going towards a worthy cause.

Children enjoy seeing their work on display. A percentage of the sale might benefit the class or the child directly in the form of class money, if the class is playing the Money Game.

Real souvenirs could be custom-made by businesses keen to advertise in this way. Spoons, mugs, plastic carry bags and T shirts, could carry the school name and symbol on one side, and the name of the sponsor on the other. The whole product could be made, supplied and delivered by the sponsor.

Such a shop lends itself to many varied activities within the school. Advertisements could be designed by the children themselves and posted around the community. Class discussion might reveal some enterprising ideas to attract media mention.

Letterbox drops too could be handled street by street around where the children live. If each child dropped ten leaflets into boxes in his/her street, in a 200 roll school you have an instant 2,000 box coverage. You also have math lesson material in the way of discussion of these numbers, of 'hit percentage', and of advertising budgeting.

Market surveys could be conducted by senior pupils to establish what products might be better chosen for inclusion. This would be a valuable lesson in what market surveys were about and how to construct and run them.

As new artwork comes in and new products are introduced, the School Souvenir Shop would have a changing feel to it which could turn out to be an attraction for parents, visitors and children..

In the event no parent can be found to run such an enterprise, children could run it themselves, much like a tuck-shop. Classes might rotate the responsibilities and might opt to only run the shop an hour a day or on Friday mornings.

At the whole school level, individual class or single family, the Money Game offers many exciting possibilities for children to get introduced to how money works in the real world. They will utilize these concepts sooner than you or they think. They will also become aware of the need for budgeting in a real sense, and hopefully will gain a better understanding of the way their particular family finances operate. It builds concepts of value, thrift and negotiation. It will also make them more socially aware and empathetic to the needs of those less well off.

Note: I thank Terry Sheffield and Helen Varney for sharing their experiences.

Ideas For 7- to 9-Year-Olds

3. USING MATH TO GET OUT OF JAIL

Get a piece of paper or cardboard and cut out 3 slits like this so it looks like a jail. Write IN on one side and OUT on the other.

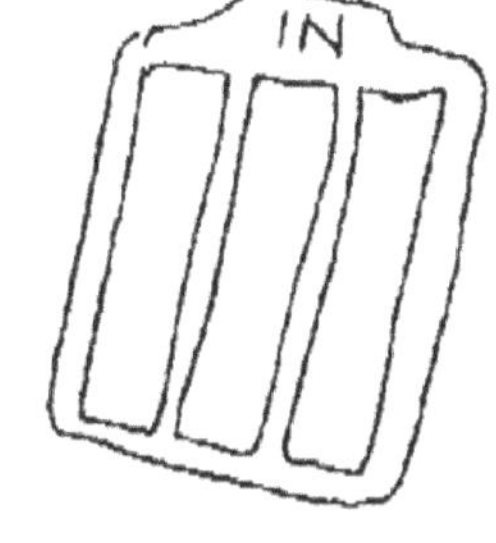

Ask somebody to hold onto one of the inside 'bars' with the word IN facing them. Say you are going to get them out of jail using your special math powers.

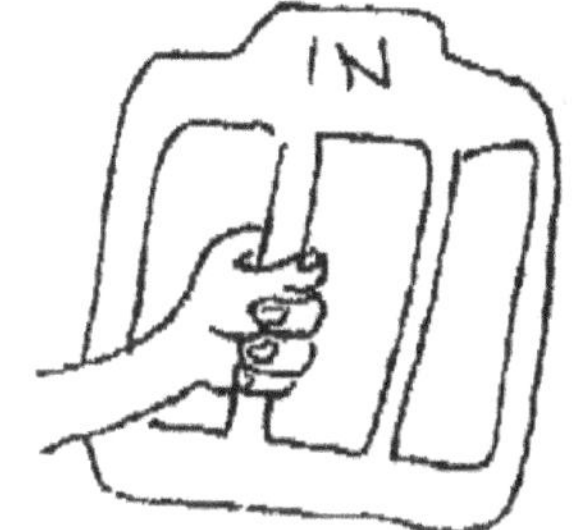

Push the bigger part into the space on the other side of the hand holding the bar. Feed that bigger end right through and out the other side. Tell him to slacken his grip so the bar can turn.

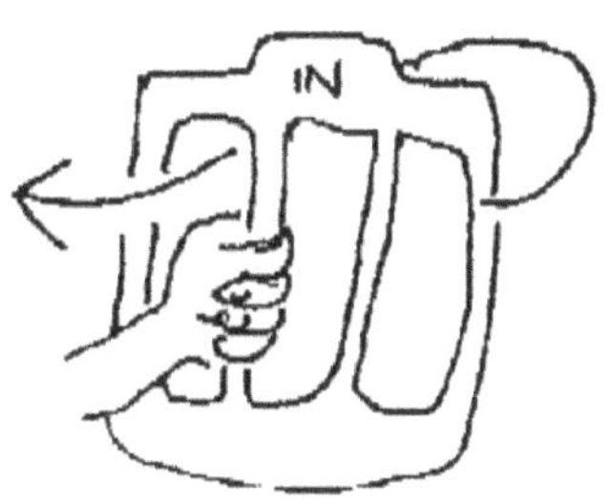

If you keep pushing it as far as it will go, the whole jail will turn inside out and end up the right way around with your friend now on the OUTSIDE!

4. YOUR FINGERS ARE CALCULATORS

FOR THE 9 TIMES TABLE

Hold your hands up facing you and pretend they are numbered from 1 to 10 like this:

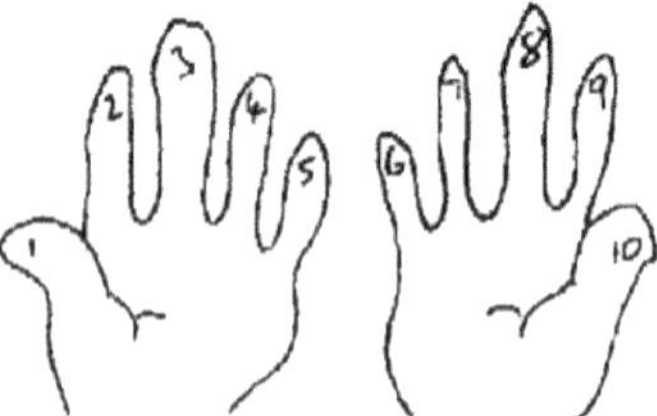

If you want to multiply say 9 x 3, you hold down the 3 finger…

…and read off the answer: 27!

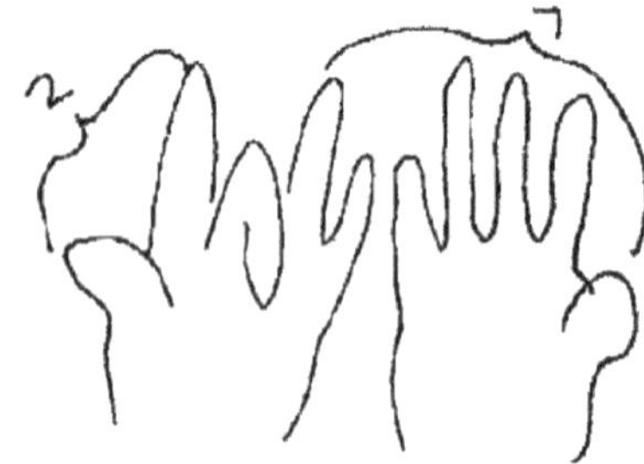

Try another one. Say 9 sevens. Fold down the 7 finger, over on the right hand, and read the answer: 6 on the left hand and 3 on the right.

YOUR FINGERS ARE CALCULATORS

FOR THE 8 TIMES TABLE

If you want say, 8 x 3, fold down the 3 finger, as before.

This time you do something else as well - whatever you're multiplying by, you fold down that many on the other side as well. So with 8 x 3, fold down the last 3 fingers as shown. Now read off the answer: 24.

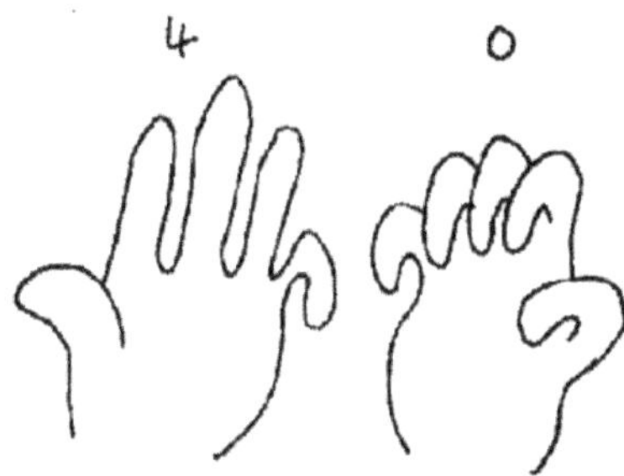

Try another one, say 8 x 5. Fold down the 5 finger on the left hand, and the last 5 on the right. The answer is four zero, or 40.

You can't do any more than 8 fives in this way. What about 8 sixes, or 7 tens? For any numbers between 6 and 10 do something else again, see next page.

YOUR FINGERS ARE CALCULATORS

FOR THE 6 TIMES - 10 TIMES TABLES

This time think of your left hand being numbered from 6 to 10 just like the right one, starting off with both little fingers which are 6.

You have to do two things - add something and multiply. Suppose you want to work out 7 x 8. Touch the 7 finger on one hand to the 8 finger on the other.

To get the answer you add across the join and those below, that makes 5. So 5 is the first figure of the answer. Then you look above the join and multiply what's on each side. On the left are 3(thumb and two fingers) and on the right are two. 3 x 2 = 6. So 6 is the second figure of the answer which is five six, or 56!

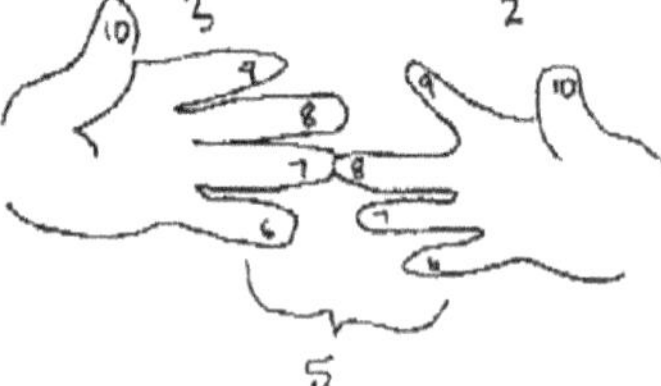

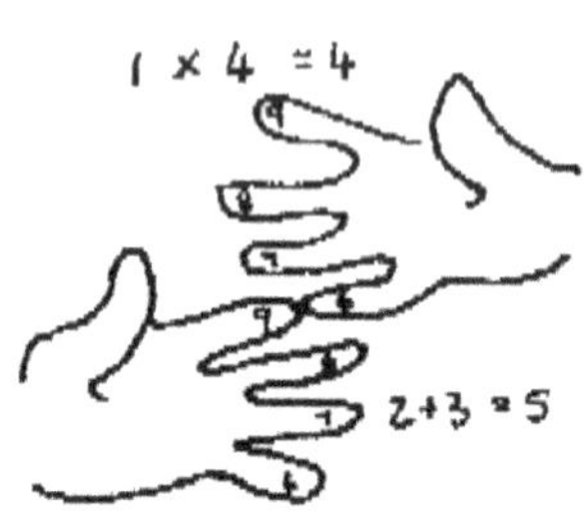

Here's another - 9 x 6. Join the 9 to the 6. Count across the join and those below and you get 5. Look above the join and multiply. You have 5 and 4. 54!

CUTTING THE APPLE

This is a more interesting way to cut an apple in half. You'll need a sharp pointed knife. And an apple! Be careful of fingers. Do it on a table or cutting board.

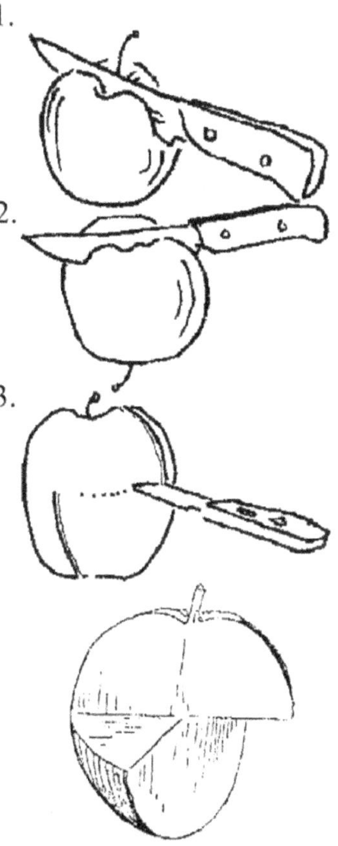

1. Make a vertical cut down to about halfway.

2. Take the knife out, turn the apple over, and turn it 90 degrees. Then cut through the bottom of the apple also down to halfway. Because you turned the apple, this cut is now at right angles to the first cut.

3. Take out the knife and turn the apple on its side. Stick the point of the apple in at the base of one line, poke it into the centre of the apple, and pull it around to the top of the other line. Take the knife out, turn the apple right around, and do the same on the other side.

Gently pull the halves apart. It should look like this. Take out the knife and gently pull the apple halves apart. It should look like this. Cor!

DID YOU KNOW…?

- The Chiquitas of Bolivia had no number words in their language.
- In France there is a village with one letter in its name. It is called Y which means there. And in Denmark there's a town called A.
- Long ago in India, the unit of measuring distance was a cow's moo. One moo was the point at which it could no longer be heard.
- The South Pole is 2,799 meters higher than the North Pole.
- When cracks appear on a sheet of glass, they move at 5,000 kilometers per hour.
- A meter is one ten millionth part of the distance between the North Pole and the Equator, passing through Paris.
- There is a sand dune in the Sahara Desert higher than the Empire State Building.
- 13 is the luckiest number in Italy.
- In Japan, 19, 33, and 42 are unlucky.
- King Mutesa of Uganda is supposed to have had 7,000 wives.
- The elephant is the only animal with 4 knees. And an elephant can weigh as much as 90 men. A blue whale can weigh as much as 1900 men.
- In 1866, 80 soldiers from the tiny country of Lichtenstein marched off to fight in the Astro-Prussian War. 81 came back. No-one could explain it.

FOR BRAINY PEOPLE

Although these mightn't come under the banner of magic, they can provide discussion just as well for small or large class groups. They are classics and have been utilized many times by math teachers over the years. I make no claim of originality for any of them: they are to be found in many old puzzle books. If you are in a teaching situation I suggest you try some, or at home they may provide interesting fireside discussions.

THE HOTEL PUZZLE

Three people check into a hotel. They pay $30 to the manager and go to their room. The manager finds out that the room rate is $25 and gives $5 to the bellboy to return. On the way to the room the bellboy reasons that $5 would be difficult to share among three people so he pockets $2 and gives $1 to each person.

Now each person paid $10 and got back $1. So they paid $9 each, totaling $27. The bellboy has $2, totaling $29. Where is the remaining dollar?

Solution: Each person paid $9, totaling $27. The manager has $25 and the bellboy $2. The bellboy's $2 should be added to the manager's $25 or subtracted from the tenants' $27, not added to the tenants' $27.

THE CAMEL PUZZLE

An Arab sheikh tells his two sons to race their camels to a distant city to see who will inherit his fortune. The one whose camel is slower will win. The brothers, after wandering aimlessly for days, ask a wise man for advice. After hearing the advice they jump on the camels and race as fast as they can to the city. What does the wise man say?

Solution: The wise man tells them to switch camels.

THE BASEBALL COMPETITION

97 baseball teams participate in an annual state tournament. The way the champion is chosen for this tournament is by the same old elimination schedule. That is, the 97 teams are to be divided into pairs, and the two teams of each pair play against each other. After a team is eliminated from each pair, the winners would be again divided into pairs, etc. How many games must be played to determine a champion?

Solution: In order to determine a winner all but one team must lose. Therefore there must be at least 96 games.

THE FLOWER PUZZLE

How many flowers do I have if all of them are roses except two, all of them are tulips except two, and all of them are daisies except two?

There are two solutions:
Three flowers: rose, tulip, daisy
Two flowers: carnation, geranium

TEA AND COFFEE

Start with a half cup of tea and a half cup of coffee. Take one tablespoon of the tea and mix it in with the coffee. Take one tablespoon of this mixture and mix it back in with the tea. Which of the two cups contains more of its original contents?

Solution: The two cups end up with the same volume of liquid they started with. The same amount of tea was moved to the coffee cup as coffee to the teacup. Therefore each cup contains the same amount of its original contents.

CROSSING THE RIVER

Three humans, one big monkey and two small monkeys are to cross a river:

a) Only humans and the big monkey can row the boat.

b) At all times, the number of humans on either side of the river must be GREATER OR EQUAL to the number of monkeys on THAT side. (Or else the humans will be eaten by the monkeys!)

Solution: The three columns represent the left bank, the boat, and the right bank respectively. The < or > indicates the direction of motion of the boat.

HHHMmm		
HHHm	Mm>	
HHHm	<M	m
HHH	Mm>	m
HHH	<M	mm
HM	HH>	mm
HM	<Hm	Hm
Hm	HM>	Hm
Hm	<Hm	HM
mm	HH>	HM
mm	<M	HHH
m	Mm>	HHH
m	<M	HHHm
	Mm>	HHHm
		HHHMmm

DAFT PUZZLES

THE BICYCLES

A man lies dead in a room with fifty-three bicycles in front of him. What happened?

In this game, a situation like the one above is presented to a group of players, who must then try to find out more about the situation by asking further questions. The person who initially presented the situation can only answer "yes" or "no" to questions (or occasionally "irrelevant" or "doesn't matter"). The sneakier and more shaggy-dog-type, the better are the tales. For instance in the above, the 'bicycles' are packs of cards.

THE ELEVATOR

A man lives on the twelfth floor of an apartment building. Every morning he takes the elevator down to the lobby and leaves the building. In the evening, he gets into the elevator, and, if there is someone else in the elevator - or if it was raining that day - he goes back to his floor directly. However, if there is nobody else in the elevator and it hasn't rained, he goes to the 10th floor and walks up two flights of stairs to his room.

Solution: The man has dwarfism. He can't reach the upper elevator buttons, but he can ask people to push them for him. He can also push them with his umbrella.

THE GUN IN THE BAR

A man walks into a bar and asks for a drink. The bartender pulls out a gun and points it at him. The man says, "Thank you," and walks out.

Solution: The man has hiccups; the bartender scares them away by pulling a gun.

THE INSOMNIAC

A man is sitting in bed. He can't sleep. So he makes a phone call, saying nothing, and then goes to sleep.

Solution: He is in a hotel, and is unable to sleep because the man in the adjacent room is snoring. He calls the room next door (from his own room number he can easily figure out his neighbor's, and from the room number, the telephone number). The snorer wakes up, answers the phone. The first man hangs up without saying anything and goes to sleep before the snorer gets back to sleep and starts snoring again.

THINGS IN A FIELD

There are a carrot, a pile of pebbles, and a pipe lying together in the middle of a field. Why?

Solution: They're the remains of a melted snowman.

THE MOTEL

It's the middle of the night. A man leaves a motel room, goes to his car to get something, and forgets which room he is in, so he honks the horn. Why?

Solution: His wife is deaf, so he honks the car horn loudly, waking up everyone else in the motel. The other residents all get up and turn on their room lights; the man then returns to the one dark room.

THE ISLAND

A man is alone on an island with no food and no water, yet he does not fear for his life.

Solution: The "island" is a traffic island.

CAN'T GO HOME

Joe wants to go home, but he can't go home because the man in the mask is waiting for him.

Solution: A baseball game is going on. The base-runner sees the catcher waiting at home plate with the ball, and so decides to stay at third base to avoid being tagged out.

THE TRAIN

A train pulls into a station, but none of the waiting passengers move.

Solution: It's a model train set.

ALL IN BLACK

A black man dressed all in black, wearing a black mask, stands at a crossroads in a totally black-painted town. All of the streetlights in town are broken. There is no moon. A black-painted car without headlights drives straight toward him, but turns in time and doesn't hit him.

Solution: It's daytime.

THE FOUR TENANTS

Bob and Carol and Ted and Alice all live in the same house. Bob and Carol go out to a movie, and when they return, Alice is lying dead on the floor in a puddle of water and glass. It is obvious that Ted killed her but Ted is not prosecuted or severely punished. Why?

Solution: Alice is a goldfish; Ted is a cat.

HAPPENED ON FRIDAY

A man rides into town on Friday. He stays one whole night and leaves on Friday.

Solution: Friday is a horse.

BORN AND DIES

A man is born in 1972 and dies in 1952 at the age of 25. How come?

Solution: He's born in room number 1972 of a hospital and dies in room number 1952.

(I did warn you they were daft)

For Geniuses Only

1. Three mathematicians, A, B, and C, are wearing hats, which they know are either black or white but not all white. A can see the hats of B and C; B can see the hats of A and C; C is blind. Each is asked in turn if they know the color of their own hat. The answers are: A: "No." B: "No." C: "Yes." What color is C's hat and how does she know?

Solution: A must see at least one black hat, or she would know that her hat is black since they are not all white. B also must see at least one black hat, and further, that hat had to be on C, otherwise she would know that her hat was black (since she knows A saw at least one black hat). So C knows that her hat is black, without even seeing the others' hats.

2. Two men stand at a fork in the road. One fork leads to Someplaceorother; the other fork leads to Nowheresville. One of these people always answers the truth to any yes/no question which is asked of him. The other always lies when asked any yes/no question. By asking one yes/no question, can you determine the road to Someplaceorother?

Solution: The fact that there are two is a red herring - you only need one of either type. You ask him the following question: "If I were to ask you if the left fork leads to Someplaceorother, would you say 'yes'?" If the person asked is a truth teller, he will answer "yes" if the left fork leads to Someplaceorother, and "no" otherwise. But so will the liar. So, either way, go left if the answer is "yes", and right otherwise.

It is possible, of course, that the liar is malicious, and he will tell the truth if he figures out that you are trying to trick him.

3. Two mathematicians place cards on their foreheads so that what is written on the card is visible only to the other logician. Consecutive positive integers have been written on the cards. The following conversation ensues: A: "I don't know my number." B: "I don't know my number." A: "I don't know my number." B: "I don't know my number." ... n statements of ignorance later ... A or B: "I know my number." What is on the card and how does the logician know it?

Solution: If A saw 1, she would know that she had 2, and would say so. Therefore, A did not see 1. A says "I don't know my number." If B saw 2, she would know that she had 3, since she knows that A did not see 1, so B did not see 1 or 2. B says "I don't know my number." If A saw 3, she would know that she had 4, since she knows that B did not see 1 or 2, so A did not see 1, 2 or 3. A says "I don't know my number." If B saw 4, she would know that she had 5, since she knows that A did not see 1, 2 or 3, so B did not see 1, 2, 3 or 4. B says "I don't know my number." . .. n statements of ignorance later ... If X saw n, she would know that she had n + 1, since she knows that ~X did not see 1 ... n - 1, so X did see n. X says "I know my number."

And the number is n + 1.

4. While three mathematicians were sleeping under a tree, a malicious child painted their heads red. Upon waking, each logician spies the child's handiwork as it applied to the heads of the other two. Naturally they start laughing. Suddenly one falls silent. Why?

Solution: The one who fell silent, presumably the quickest of the three, reasoned that his head must be painted also. The argument goes as follows. Let's call the quick one Q, and the other two D and S. Let's assume Q's head is untouched. Then D is laughing because S's head is painted, and vice versa. But eventually, D and S will realize that their head must be painted, because the other is laughing. So they will quit laughing as soon as they realize this. So, Q waits what he thinks is a reasonable amount of time for them to figure this out, and when they don't stop laughing, his worst fears are confirmed. He concludes that his assumption is invalid and he must be crowned in crimson too.

5. A very bright and sunny Day The Priest did to the Verger say: "Last Monday met I strangers three, None of which were

known to Thee. I ask'd Them of Their Age combin'd which amounted twice to Thine! A Riddle now will I give Thee: Tell Me what Their Ages be!"

So the Verger ask'd the Priest: "Give to Me a Clue at least!" "Keep Thy Mind and Ears awake, And see what Thou of this can make. Their Ages multiplied make plenty, Fifty and Ten Dozens Twenty."

The Verger had a sleepless Night To try to get Their Ages right. "I almost found the Answer right. Please shed on it a little Light." "A little Clue I give to Thee, I'm older than all Strangers three." After but a little While The Verger answered with a Smile: "Inside my Head has rung a Bell. Now I know the answer well!"

Now, the question is: How old is the PRIEST?

Solution: The puzzler tried to take the test; Intriguing rhymes he wished to best. But "Fifty and ten dozens twenty" made his headache pound aplenty. When he finally found some leisure, He took to task this witty treasure.

"The product of the age must be Twenty-Four Hundred Fifty!" Knowing that, he took its primes, permuted them as many times as needed, 'til he found amounts equal to, by all accounts, twice the Verger's age, so that He would have that next day's spat.

The reason for the lad's confusion was due to multiple solution! Hence he needed one more clue to give the answer back to you! Since only one could fit the bill, and then confirm the priest's age still, the eldest age of each solution by one could differ, with no coercion.

Else, that last clue's revelation, would not have brought information! With two, two, five, seven, and seven, construct three ages, another set of seven. Two sets of three yield sixty-four, Examine them, yet one time more. The eldest age of each would be forty-nine, and then, fifty!

With lack of proper rhyme and meter, I've tried to be the first completer of this poem and a puzzle; my poetry, you'd try to muzzle! And lest you think my wit is thrifty, The answer, of course, must be fifty! If dispute, you wish to tender, note my address, as the sender!

6. You have ten identical looking bags; each contains nine coins. The coins in one bag weigh 0.9g each - they are counterfeit, and the rest in the other bags are real - they weigh 1.0g. You have **ONE** weighing on a VERY accurate scale to find the bag containing the counterfeit coins. Even *you* don't know which bag it is. (they can be shuffled around into any order) How do you solve it?

Solution: Arbitrarily number the bags 0-9. Take 0 coins from bag 0, 1 coin from bag 1, 2 coins from bag 2, etc. Now weigh all those selected coins and follow this table:

If counterfeit bag is	Final weight is
0	45g
1	44.9g
2	44.8g
3	44.7g
4	44.6g

5	44.5g
6	44.4g
7	44.3g
8	44.2g
9	44.1g

ACKNOWLEDGEMENTS

I would like to thank Claire Aumonier, for the frequent inspirational and passionate discussions we had on this subject. I am grateful too to Larry Moss in the USA, Terry Sheffield in Northland, and Helen Varney for contributing of their ideas and experiences, also to the late Harry Eng in San Diego, and Mary Crockett and Bridget Nash for letting me bounce back ideas. Thanks to the NZ government for awarding me a QEII Award in 1992 for services in schools. And the biggest thank you to the many parents and school administrators up and down this country who booked my MATHMAN! shows and seminars between 1988-2005.

OTHER CONTRIBUTORS

Laura Almasy , Ranjit S. Bhatnagar, Chris Cole, Matt Crawford, Matthew William Daly, Ken Duisenberg, Sylvia Dutcher, Marguerite Eisenstein, Thomas Freeman, Andreas Gammel, Joaquin Hartman, Marcy Hartman, Karl Heuer, Geoff Hopcraft, David Huddleston, Mark Isaak, Steve Jacquot , J|rgen Jensen, Karen Karp, Nev King, Shelby Kilmer, Ken Largman, Andy Latto, Howard Lazoff, Merlyn LeRoy, Dan Murray, Ted McCabe, Jim Moskowitz, Damian Mulvena, Jan Mark Noworolski, Peter R. Olpe, Martin Pitwood, Charles Renert, Ellen M. Sentovich, Annie Senghas, Eric Stephan, Diana Stiefbold, Simon Travaglia, David Van Stone, Randy Whitaker, Matthew P Wiener, Kevin Nechodom, .

BOOKS:

Beasley, John, *The Mathematics of Games,* Oxford University Press 1989

Bergamini, David, *Mathematics*, Time/Life International 1965

Burgess, G, *The Purple Cow and Other Nonsense*, Dover 1961

Gardner, M, *Mathematical Carnival*, Alfred Knopf, 1975

Illich, I, *Deschooling Society*, Penguin 1971

Paulos, John Allen, *Innumeracy*, Hill and Wang 1988

Rogers, Agnes, *How Come?* Doubleday & Company, Inc., New York, 1953

Sloane, Paul, *Lateral Thinking Puzzlers*, Sterling Publishing Co. Inc. 1992

Weintraub, Richard & Krieger, Richard, *Beyond the Easy Answer*, Zenger Publications Inc, 1979

ARTICLES:

D. O'Connor, "Pragmatic Paradoxes," *Mind* 57:358-9, 1948.

J. Bennett and J. Cargile, Reviews, *J Symb. Logic* 30:101-3, 1965.

R. Binkley, "The Surprise Examination in Modal Logic," *J Phil* 65:127-36, 1968.

C. Harrison, "The Unanticipated Examination in View of Kripke's Semantics for Modal Logic," in *Philosophical Logic*, J. Davis et al (ed.), Dordrecht, 1969.

P. Windt, "The Liar in the Prediction Paradox," *Am Phil* Q 10:65-8, 1973.

A. Ayer, "On a Supposed Antinomy," Mind 82:125-6, 1973.

J. Muncy "Thoughts on Homeschooling"

P. F. Kanter, Brian A. Griffin "Helping Your Child Learn Math" US Dept of Education 1994

Asimov, Isaac, "The Relativity of Wrong", Skeptical Inquirer 1989.

MATH PATTERNS

0 x 9+1 = 1
1 x 9+2 = 11
12 x 9+3 = 111
123 x 9+1 = 1111
1234 x 9+1 = 11111
12345 x 9+1 = 111111
123456 x 9+1 = 1111111
1234567 x 9+1 = 11111111
12345678 x 9+1 = 111111111

0 x 9+3 = 3
3 x 9+6 = 33
36 x 9+9 = 333
369 x 9+12 = 3333

0 x 9+2 = 2
2 x 9+4 = 22
24 x 9+6 = 222
246 x 9+8 = 2222
2468 x 9+10 = 22222

0 x 9+8=8
9 x 9+7=88
98 x 9+6=888
987 x 9+5=8888
9876 x 9+4=88888
98765 x 9+3=888888
987654 x 9+2=8888888
9876543 x 9+1=88888888
98765432 x 9+0=888888888
987654321 x 9-1=8888888888
9876543210 x 9-2=88888888888

1 = 1 = 1
1+2+1 = 4 = 2
1+2+3+2+1 = 9 = 3
1+2+3+4+3+2+1 =16 = 4
1+2+3+4+5+4+3+2+1 = 25 = 5
1+2+3+4+5+6+5+4+3+2+1 = 36 = 6
1+2+3+4+5+6+7+6+5+4+3+2+1 = 49 = 7
1+2+3+4+5+6+7+8+7+6+5+4+3+2+1 = 64 = 8
1+2+3+4+5+6+7+8+9+8+7+6+5+4+3+2+1 = 81 = 9
1+2+3+4+5+6+7+8+9+10+9+8+7+6+5+4+3+2+1 =100 = 10
1+2+3+4+5+6+7+8+9+10+11+10+9+8+7+6+5+4+3+2+1 = 121 = 11
1+2+3+4+5+6+7+8+9+10+11+12+11+10+9+8+7+6+5+4+3+2+1 = 144 = 12

12345679 X 9 = 111111111
12345679 X 18 = 222222222
12345679 X 27 = 333333333
12345679 X 36 = 444444444

12345679 X 81 = 999999999

142857 X 1 = 142857
142857 X 2 = 285714
142857 X 3 = 428571
142857 X 4 = 571428
142857 X 5 = 714285
142857 X 6 = 857142

(Answer repeats in the same order)

987654321	123456789
87654321	12345678
7654321	1234567
654321	123456
54321	12345
4321	1234
321	123
21	12
1	1

Both sides add to the same answer: 1,083,676,269

1 x 8+1=9
12 x 8+2=98
123 x 8+3=987
1234 x 8+4=9876
12345 x 8+5=98765
123456 x 8+6=987654
1234567 x 8+7=9876543
12345678 x 8+8=98765432
123456789 x 8+9=987654321

1 x 1	=	1
11 x 11	=	121
111 x 111	=	12321
1111 x 1111	=	1234321
11111 x 11111	=	123454321
111111 x 111111	=	12345654321
1111111 x 1111111	=	1234567654321
11111111 x 11111111	=	123456787654321
111111111 x 111111111	=	12345678987654321

3 x 37037 = 111111
6 x 37037 = 222222
9 x 37037 = 333333
12 x 37037 = 444444
15 x 37037 = 555555
18 x 37037 = 666666
21 x 37037 = 777777
24 x 37037 = 888888
27 x 37037 = 999999

19 x 1 = 19 and 1 + 9 = 10 and 1 + 0 = 1
19 x 2 = 38 " 3 + 8 = 11 " 1 + 1 = 2
19 x 3 = 57 " 5 + 7 = 12 " 1 + 2 = 3
19 x 4 = 76 " 7 + 6 = 13 " 1 + 3 = 4
19 x 5 = 95 " 9 + 5 = 14 " 1 + 4 = 5
19 x 6 = 114 " 11 + 4=15 " 1 + 5 = 6
19 x 7 = 133 " 13 + 3=16 " 1 + 6 = 7
19 x 8 = 152 " 15 + 2=17 " 1 + 7 = 8
19 x 9 = 171 " 17 + 1=18 " 1 + 8 = 9
19 x 10=190 " 19 + 0= 19 " 1 + 9 = 10

9109 x 1 = 09109 add digits = 19
9109 x 2 = 18218 " " = 20
9109 x 3 = 27327 " " = 21
9109 x 4 = 36436 " " = 22
9109 x 5 = 45545 " " = 23
9109 x 6 = 54654 " " = 24
9109 x 7 = 63763 " " = 25
9109 x 8 = 72872 " " = 26
9109 x 9 = 81981 " " = 27

Note how
these columns
run from 0-9
and 9-1

(courtesy of Bay Of Plenty Times, Oct 13th, 1993)

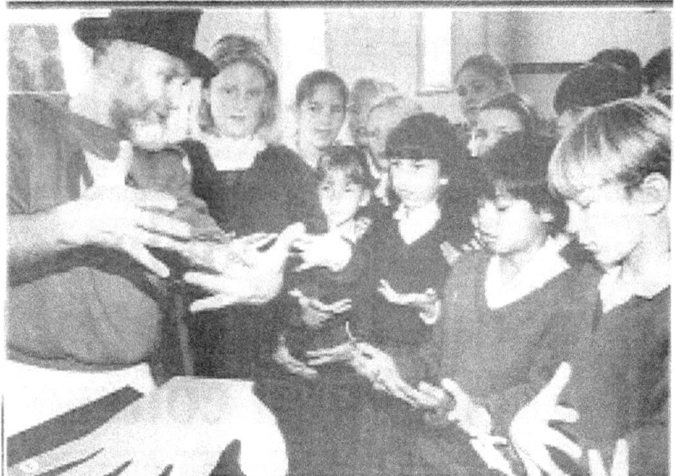

Pupils see the magic of maths

By Val Sherriff

COUNT on your brain not your eyes, but multiply on your fingers, Bethlehem College pupils were told yesterday by visiting Mathman Ken Ring.

In three hour-long sessions the caped crusader and magician who upholds proof, justice and the numerical way showed students how to multiply on fingers and demonstrated some of the weird and wonderful ways numbers behaved.

Mathman's mission is to show that maths is not boring. Formerly a primary school teacher, Mr Ring metamorphosised into Mathman five years ago.

The combination of magic and mathematics is a powerful one, Mr Ring said.

Until children are a certain age they believe everything is magic. Older children are capable of using mathematical concepts to work things out.

His show, a mixture of magic tricks, jokes and riddles transfixed his participating audience.

One child said she had enjoyed his clock which went backwards.

Black caped, top hatted, with a blue sweatshirt embossed with a large M, Mathman said he dressed up to gain the children's attention.

www.ingramcontent.com/pod-product-compliance
Lightning Source LLC
Chambersburg PA
CBHW031317040426
42443CB00005B/114

9780864670007